PIONEERS OF EVOLUTION

Hon. John Collier. pinx.

C. Darwin.

PIONEERS OF EVOLUTION
FROM THALES TO HUXLEY

WITH AN INTERMEDIATE CHAPTER ON
THE CAUSES OF ARREST OF THE MOVEMENT

BY

EDWARD CLODD

WITH PORTRAITS

Essay Index Reprint Series

BOOKS FOR LIBRARIES PRESS
FREEPORT, NEW YORK

First Published 1897
Reprinted 1972

Library of Congress Cataloging in Publication Data

Clodd, Edward, 1840-1930.
  Pioneers of evolution from Thales to Huxley.

  (Essay index reprint series)
  Reprint of the 1897 ed.
  1. Evolution--History. 2. Philosophy--History.
3. Spencer, Herbert, 1820-1903. 4. Huxley, Thomas
Henry, 1825-1895. I. Title.
QH361.C58 1972   575'.009   74-37470
ISBN 0-8369-2540-8

PRINTED IN THE UNITED STATES OF AMERICA
BY
NEW WORLD BOOK MANUFACTURING CO., INC.
HALLANDALE, FLORIDA 33009

TO MY BELOVED

A. A. L.

WHOSE FELLOWSHIP AND HELP

HAVE SWEETENED LIFE.

PREFACE.

THIS book needs only brief introduction. It attempts to tell the story of the origin of the Evolution idea in Ionia, and, after long arrest, of the revival of that idea in modern times, when its profound and permanent influence on thought in all directions, and, therefore, on human relations and conduct, is apparent.

Between birth and revival there were the centuries of suspended animation, when the nepenthe of dogma drugged the reason; the Church teaching, and the laity mechanically accepting, the sufficiency of the Scriptures and of the General Councils to decide on matters which lie outside the domain of both. Hence the necessity for particularizing the causes which actively arrested advance in knowledge for sixteen hundred years.

In indicating the parts severally played in the Renascence of Evolution by a small group of illustrious men, the writer, through the courtesy of Mr.

Herbert Spencer, has been permitted to see the original documents which show that the theory of Evolution as a whole; i. e., as dealing with the non-living, as well as with the living, contents of the Universe, was formulated by Mr. Spencer in the year preceding the publication of the Origin of Species.

ROSEMONT, TUFNELL PARK, LONDON, N.,
14th December, 1896.

CONTENTS.

PART I.

vii

" Nature, which governs the whole, will soon change all things which thou seest, and out of their substance will make other things, and again other things from the substance of them, in order that the world may be ever new."

Marcus Aurelius, vii, 25.

PIONEERS OF EVOLUTION.

PART I.

PIONEERS OF EVOLUTION FROM THALES TO LUCRETIUS.

B. C. 600–A. D. 50.

" These all died in faith, not having received the promises, but having seen them afar off, and were persuaded of them."—HE-BREWS xi. 13.

" ONE event is always the son of another, and we must never forget the parentage," said a Bechuana chief to Casalis the missionary. The barbarian philosopher spoke wiser than he knew, for in his words lay that doctrine of continuity and unity which is the creed of modern science. They are a suitable text to the discourse of this chapter, the design of which is to bring out what the brilliancy of present-day discoveries tends to throw into shadow, namely, the antiquity of the ideas of which those discoveries are the result. Although the Theory of Evolution, as we define it, is new, the speculations which made it possible are, at least, twenty-five centuries old. Indeed, it is not practicable, since the remote past yields no documents, to fix their beginnings. Moreover, charged, as they are, with many crudities, they are not detachable from the barbaric conceptions of the Universe which are the philosophies of past, and the legends of present, times.

Fontenelle, a writer of the last century, shrewdly remarked that " all nations made the astounding part of their myths while they were savage, and retained them from custom and religious conservatism." For, as Walter Bagehot argues in his brilliant little book on Physics and Politics, and as all anthropological research goes to prove, the lower races are non-progressive both through fear and instinct. And the majority of the members of higher races have not escaped from the operation of the same causes. Hence the persistence of coarse and grotesque elements in speculations wherein man has made gradual approach to the truth of things; hence, too— the like phenomena having to be interpreted—the similarity of the explanation of them. And as primitive myth embodies primitive theology, primitive morals, and primitive science, the history of beliefs shows how few there be who have escaped from the tyranny of that authority and sanctity with which the lapse of time invests old ideas.

Dissatisfaction is a necessary condition of progress; and dissatisfaction involves opposition. As Grant Allen puts it, in one of his most felicitous poems:

> If systems that be are the order of God,
> Revolt is a part of the order.

Hence a stage in the history of certain peoples when, in questioning what is commonly accepted, intellectual freedom is born. Such a stage was markedly reached whenever, for example, an individual here and there challenged the current belief about the beginnings and nature of things, beliefs held because they were taught, not because their correspondence with fact had been examined.

A pioneer (French, *pionnier;* Italian, *pedone; from Latin *pedes*) is, literally, a foot-soldier; one who goes before an army to clear the road of obstructions. Hence the application of the term to men who are in the van of any new movement; hence its special fitness in the present connection, as designating men whose speculations cut a pathway through jungles of myth and legend to the realities of things. The Pioneers of Evolution—the first on record to doubt the truth of the theory of special creation, whether as the work of departmental gods or of one Supreme Deity, matters not—lived in Greece about the time already mentioned; six centuries before Christ. Not in the early stages of the Evolution idea, in the Greece limited, as now, to a rugged peninsula in the southeastern corner of Europe and to the surrounding islands, but in the Greece which then included Ionia, on the opposite seaboard of Asia Minor.

From times beyond memory or record, the islands of the Ægean had been the nurseries of culture and adventure. Thence the maritime inhabitants had spread themselves both east and west, feeding the spirit of inquiry, and imbibing influences from

older civilizations, notably of Egypt and Chaldæa.
But, mix as they might with other peoples, the
Greeks never lost their own strongly marked indi-
viduality, and, in imparting what they had acquired
or discovered to younger peoples, that is, younger
in culture, they stamped it with an impress all their
own.

At the later period with which we are dealing,
refugees from the Peloponnesus, who would not submit to the Dorian yoke, had been long settled in
Ionia. To what extent they had been influenced
by contact with their neighbours is a question which,
even were it easy to answer, need not occupy us
here. Certain it is that trade and travel had widened
their intellectual horizon, and although India lay too
remote to touch them closely (if that incurious,
dreamy East had touched them, it would have taught
them nothing), there was Babylonia with her star-
watchers, and Egypt with her land-surveyors. From
the one, these Ionians probably gained knowledge
of certain periodic movements of some of the heavenly bodies; and from the other, a few rules of
mensuration, perchance a little crude science. But
this is conjecture. For all the rest that she evolved,
and with which she enriched the world, ancient
Greece is in debt to none.

While the Oriental shrunk from quest after
causes, looking, as Professor Butcher aptly remarks
in his Aspects of the Greek Genius, on " each fresh
gain of earth as so much robbery of heaven," the

Greek eagerly sought for the law governing the facts around him. And in Ionia was born the idea foreign to the East, but which has become the starting-point of all subsequent scientific inquiry—the idea that Nature works by fixed laws. Sir Henry Maine said that "except the blind forces of Nature, nothing moves which is not Greek in its origin," and we feel how hard it is to avoid exaggeration when speaking of the heritage bequeathed by Greece as the giver of every fruitful, quickening idea which has developed human faculty on all sides, and enriched every province of life. Amid serious defects of character, as craftiness, avariciousness, and unscrupulousness, the Greeks had the redeeming grace of pursuit after knowledge which naught could baffle (Plato, Republic, vol. iv, p. 435), and that healthy outlook on things which saved them from morbid introspection. There arose among them no Simeon Stylites to mount his profitless pillar; no filth-ingrained fakir to waste life in contemplating the tip of his nose; no schoolman to idly speculate how many angels could dance upon a needle's point; or to debate such fatuous questions as the language which the saints in heaven will speak after the Last Judgment.

In his excellent and cautious survey of Early Greek Philosophy, which we mainly follow in this section, Professor Burnet says that the real advance made by the Ionians was through their "leaving off telling tales. They gave up the hopeless task of describing what was when as yet there was nothing,

and asked instead what all things really are now."
For the early notions of the Greeks about nature,
being an inheritance from their barbaric ancestors,
were embodied in myths and legends bearing strong
resemblance to those found among the uncivilized
tribes of Polynesia and elsewhere in our day. For
example, the old nature-myth of Cronus separating
heaven and earth by the mutilation of Uranus occurs
among Chinese, Japanese, and Maoris, and among
the ancient Hindus and Egyptians.

The earliest school of scientific speculation was
at Miletus, the most flourishing city of Ionia. Thales,
whose name heads the list of the " Seven Sages,"
was its founder. As with other noted philosophers
of this and later periods, neither the exact date of his
birth nor of his death are known, but the sixth
century before Christ may be held to cover the period
when he " flourished."

That " nothing comes into being out of nothing,
and that nothing passes away into nothing," was the
conviction with which he and those who followed
him started on their quest. All around was change;
everything always becoming something else; " all in
motion like streams." There must be that which is
the vehicle of all the changes, and of all the motions
which produce them. *What*, therefore, was this permanent and primary substance? in other words, of
what is the world made? And Thales, perhaps
through observing that it could become vaporous,
liquid, and solid in turn; perhaps—if, as tradition

records, he visited Egypt—through watching the
wonder-working, life-giving Nile; perhaps as doubtless sharing the current belief in an ocean-washed
earth, said that the primary substance was WATER.
Anaximander, his friend and pupil, disagreeing with
what seemed to him a too concrete answer, argued,
in more abstract fashion, that "the material cause
and first element of things was the Infinite." This
material cause, which he was the first thus to name,
"is neither water nor any other of what are now
called the *elements*" (we quote from Theophrastus,
the famous pupil of Aristotle, born at Eresus in Lesbos, 371 B. C.). Perhaps, following Professor Burnet's able guidance through the complexities of defi-
nitions, the term BOUNDLESS best expresses the
"one eternal, indestructible substance out of which
everything arises, and into which everything once
more returns"; in other words, the exhaustless stock
of matter from which the waste of existence is being
continually made good.

Anaximander was the first to assert the origin of
life from the non-living, i. e., "the moist element as
it was evaporated by the sun," and to speak of man
as "like another animal, namely, a fish, in the beginning." This looks well-nigh akin to prevision of
the mutability of species, and of what modern biology
has proved concerning the marine ancestry of the
highest animals, although it is one of many ancient
speculations as to the origin of life in slimy matter.
And when Anaximander adds that "while other

animals quickly find food for themselves, man alone requires a prolonged period of suckling," he anticipates the modern explanation of the origin of the rudimentary family through the development of the social instincts and affections. The lengthening of the period of infancy involves dependence on the parents, and evolves the sympathy which lies at the base of social relations. (Cf. Fiske's Outlines of Cosmic Philosophy, vol. ii, pp. 344, 360.)

In dealing with speculations so remote, we have to guard against reading modern meanings into writings produced in ages whose limitations of knowledge were serious, and whose temper and standpoint are wholly alien to our own. For example, shrewd as are some of the guesses made by Anaximander, we find him describing the sun as " a ring twenty-eight times the size of the earth, like a cartwheel with the felloe hollow and full of fire, showing the fire at a certain point, as if through the nozzle of a pair of bellows." And if he made some approach to truer ideas of the earth's shape as " convex and round," the world of his day, as in the days of Homer, thought of it as flat and as floating on the all-surrounding water. The Ionian philosophers lacked not insight, but the scientific method of starting with working hypotheses, or of observation before theory, was as yet unborn.

In this brief survey of the subject there will be no advantage in detailing the various speculations which followed on the heels of those of Thales and

Anaximander, since these varied only in non-essentials; or, like that of Pythagoras and his school, which Zeller regards as the outcome of the teachings of Anaximander, were purely abstract and fanciful. As is well known, the Pythagoreans, whose philosophy was ethical as well as cosmical, held that all things are made of numbers, each of which they believed had its special character and property. A belief in such symbols as entities seems impossible to us, but its existence in early thought is conceivable when, as Aristotle says, they were "not separated from the objects of sense." Even in the present day, among the eccentric people who still believe in the modern sham agnosticism, known as theosophy, and in astrology, we find the delusion that numbers possess inherent magic or mystic virtues. So far as the ancients are concerned, "consider," as Mr. Benn remarks in his Greek Philosophers (vol. i, p. 12), "the lively emotions excited at a time when multiplication and division, squaring and cubing, the rule of three, the construction and equivalence of figures, with all their manifold applications to industry, commerce, fine arts, and tactics, were just as strange and wonderful as electrical phenomena are to us . . . and we shall cease to wonder that a mere form of thought, a lifeless abstraction, should once have been regarded as the solution of every problem; the cause of all existence; or that these speculations were more than once revived in after ages."

Xenophanes of Colophon, one of the twelve

2

Ionian cities of Asia Minor, deserves, however, a passing reference. He, with Parmenides and Zeno, are the chief representatives of the Eleatic school, so named from the city in southwestern Italy where a Greek colony had settled. Then tendency of that school was toward metaphysical theories. He was the first known observer to detect the value of fossils as evidences of the action of water, but his chief claim to notice rests on the fact that, passing beyond the purely physical speculations of the Ionian school, he denied the idea of a primary substance, and theorized about the nature and actions of superhuman beings. Living at a time when there was a revival of old and gross superstitions to which the vulgar had recourse when fears of invasions arose, he dared to attack the old and persistent ideas about the gods, as in the following sentences from the fragments of his writings:

"Homer and Hesiod have ascribed to the gods all things that are a shame and a disgrace among men, theft and adulteries and deception of one another."

"There never was nor will be a man who has clear certainty as to what I say about the gods and about all things; for even if he does chance to say what is right, yet he himself does not know that it is so. But all are free to guess."

"Mortals think that the gods were born as they are, and have senses and a voice and body like their own. So the Ethiopians make their gods black and snub-nosed; the Thracians give theirs red hair and blue eyes."

" There is one god, the greatest among gods and men, unlike mortals both in mind and body."

Had such heresies been spoken in Athens, where the effects of a religious revival were still in force, the " secular arm " of the archons would probably have made short work of Xenophanes. But in Elea, or in whatever other colony he may have lived, " the gods were left to take care of themselves."

Greater than the philosophers yet named is Heraclitus of Ephesus, nicknamed " the dark," from the obscurity of his style. His original writings have shared the fate of most documents of antiquity, and exist, like many of these, only in fragments preserved in the works of other authors. Many of his aphorisms are indeed dark sayings, but those that yield their meaning are full of truth and suggestiveness. As for example:

" The eyes are more exact witnesses than the ears."

" You will not find out the boundaries of soul by travelling in any direction."

" Man is kindled and put out like a light in the nighttime."

" Man's character is his fate."

But these have special value as keys to his philosophy:

" You cannot step twice into the same rivers; for fresh waters are ever flowing in upon you."

"Homer was wrong in saying: 'Would that strife might perish from among gods and men!' He did not see that he was praying for the destruction of the universe; for, if his prayer were heard, all things would pass away."

Flux or movement, says Heraclitus, is the all-pervading law of things, and in the opposition of forces, by which things are kept going, there is underlying harmony. Still on the quest after the primary substance whose manifestations are so various, he found it in FIRE, since "the quantity of it in a flame burning steadily appears to remain the same; the flames seems to be what we call a 'thing.' And yet the substance of it is continually changing. It is always passing away in smoke, and its place is always being taken by fresh matter from the fuel that feeds it. This is just what we want. If we regard the world as an 'ever-living fire'—'this order, which is the same in all things, and which no one of gods or men has made'—we can understand how fire is always becoming all things, while all things are always returning to it." And as is the world, so is man, made up, like it, both soul and body, of the fire, the water, and the earth. We are and are not the same for two consecutive moments; "the fire in us is perpetually becoming water, and the water earth, but as the opposite process goes on simultaneously we appear to remain the same."

As speculation advanced, it became more and more applied to details, theories of the beginnings of life being followed by theories of the origin of its various forms. This is a feature of the philosophy of Empedocles, who flourished in the fifth century B. C. The advance of Persia westward had led to migrations of Greeks to the south of Italy and Sicily, and it was at Agrigentum, in that island, that Empedocles was born about 490. He has an honoured place among the earliest who supplanted *guesses* about the world by *inquiry* into the world itself. Many legends are told of his magic arts, one of which, it will be remembered, Matthew Arnold makes an occasion of some fine reflections in his poem Empedocles in Etna. The philosopher was said to have brought back to life a woman who apparently had been dead for thirty days. As he ascends the mountain, Pausanias of Gela, with an address to whom the poem of Empedocles opens, would fain have his curiosity slaked as to this and other marvels reported of him:

> Ask not the latest news of the last miracle,
> Ask not what days and nights
> In trance Pantheia lay,
> But ask how thou such sights
> May'st see without dismay ;
> Ask what most helps when known, thou son of Anchitus.

His speculations about things, like those of Parmenides before him and of Lucretius after him, are set down in verse. From the remains of his Poem on Nature we learn that he conceived " the four roots of all things " to be FIRE, AIR, EARTH, and WATER. They are " fools, lacking far-reaching thoughts, who deem that what before was not comes into being, or that aught can perish and be utterly destroyed." Therefore the "roots" or elements are eternal and indestructible. They are acted upon by two forces, which are also material, LOVE and STRIFE; the one a uniting agent, the other a disrupting agent. From the four roots, thus operated upon, arise " the colours and forms" of living things; trees first, both male and female, then fragmentary parts of animals, heads without necks, and "eyes that strayed up and down in want of a forehead," which, combined together, produced monstrous forms. These, lacking power to propagate, perished, and were replaced by "whole-natured" but sexless "forms" which "arose from the earth," and which, as Strife gained the upper hand, became male and female. Herein, amidst much fantastic speculation, would appear to be the germ of the modern theory that the unadapted become extinct, and that only the adapted survive. Nature kills off her failures to make room for her successes.

Anaxagoras, who was a contemporary of Empedocles, interests us because he was the first philosopher to repair to Athens, and the first sufferer for truth's sake of whom we have record in Greek annals. Because he taught that the sun was a red-hot stone, and that the moon had plains and ravines in it, he was put upon his trial, and but for the influence of his friend, the famous Pericles, might have suffered death. Speculations, however bold they be, pass unheeded till they collide with the popular creed, and in thus attacking the gods, attack a seemingly divinely settled order. Athens then, and long after, while indifferent about natural science, was, under the influence of the revival referred to above, actively hostile to free thinking. The opinions of Anaxagoras struck at the existence of the gods and emptied Olympus. If the sky was but an air-filled space, what became of Zeus? if the sun was only a fiery ball, what became of Apollo? Mr. Grote says (History of Greece, vol. i, p. 466) that " in the view of the early Greek, the description of the sun, as given in a modern astronomical treatise, would have appeared not merely absurd, but repulsive and impious; even in later times, Anaxagoras and other astronomers incurred the charge of blasphemy for dispersonifying Hēlios." Of Socrates, who was himself condemned to death for impiety in denying old gods and introducing news ones, the same authority writes: " Physics and astronomy, in his opinion, belonged to the divine class of phenomena, in which human research was insane, fruitless, and impious." So Demos and his " betters " clung, as the majority still cling, to the myths of their forefathers. They repaired to the oracles, and watched for the will of the gods in signs and omens.

In his philosophy Anaxagoras held that there was a portion of everything in everything, and that things are variously mixed in infinite numbers of seeds, each after its kind. From these, through the

action of an external cause, called NOUS, which also
is material, although the " thinnest of all things and
the purest," and " has power over all things," there
arose plants and animals.   It is probable, as Professor Burnet remarks, " that Anaxagoras substituted
NOUS, still conceived as a body, for the LOVE and
STRIFE of Empedocles simply because he wished
to retain the old Ionic doctrine of a substance that
' knows' all things, and to identify this with the
new theory of a substance that ' moves' all things."

Thus far speculation has run largely on the origin of life forms, but now we find revival of speculation about the nature of things generally, and the
formulation of a theory which links Greek cosmology
with early nineteenth-century science with Dalton's
ATOMIC THEORY.   Democritus of Abdera, who was
born about 460 B. C., has the credit of having elaborated an atomic theory, but probably he only further
developed what Leucippus had taught before him.
Of this last-named philosopher nothing whatever is
known; indeed, his existence has been doubted, but
it counts for something that Aristotle gives him the
credit of the discovery, and that Theophrastus, in
the first book of his Opinions, wrote of Leucippus as
follows: " He assumed innumerable and ever-mov-
ing elements, namely, the atoms.   And he made their
forms infinite in number, since there was no reason
why they should be of one kind rather than another,
and because he saw that there was unceasing becoming and change in things.   He held, further, that

what is is no more real than *what is not*, and that
both are alike causes of the things that come into
being; for he laid down that the substance of the
atoms was compact and full, and he called them
what is, while they moved in the void which he called
what is not, but affirmed to be just as real as *what is*."
Thus did " he answer the question that Thales had
been the first to ask."

Postponing further reference to this theory until
the great name of Lucretius, its Roman exponent, is
reached, we find a genuine scientific method making
its first start in the person of Aristotle. This remarkable man, the founder of the experimental school,
and the Father of Natural History, was born 384
B. C. at Stagira in Macedonia. In his eighteenth
year he left his native place for Athens, where he
became a pupil of Plato. Disappointed, as it is
thought, at not succeeding his master in the Academy, he removed to Mytilene in the island of Lesbos,
where he received an invitation from Philip of Mace-
don to become tutor to his son, the famous Alexander the Great. When Alexander went on his expedition to Asia, Aristotle returned to Athens, teaching in the " school" which his genius raised to the
first rank. There he wrote the greater part of his
works, the completion of some of which was stopped
by his death at Chalcis in 322. The range of his
studies was boundless, but in this brief notice we
must limit our survey—and the more so because Aristotle's speculations outside natural history abound in

errors—to his pioneer work in organic evolution. Here, in the one possible method of reaching the truth, theory follows observation. Stagira lay on the Strymonic gulf, and a boyhood spent by the seashore gave Aristotle ample opportunity for noting the variations, and withal gradations, between marine plants and animals, among which last-named it should be noted as proof of his insight that he was keen enough to include sponges. Here was laid the foundation of a classification of life-forms on which all corresponding attempts were based. Then, he saw, as none other before him had seen, and as none after him saw for centuries, the force of heredity, that still unsolved problem of biology. Speaking broadly of his teaching, the details of which would fill pages, its main features are (1) His insistence on observation. In his History of Animals he says " we must not accept a general principle from logic only, but must prove its application to each fact. For it is in facts that we must seek general principles, and these must always accord with facts. Experience furnishes the particular facts from which induction is the pathway to general laws." (2) His rejection of chance and assertion of law, not, following a common error, of law personified as cause, but as the term by which we express the fact that certain phenomena always occur in a certain order. In his Physics Aristotle says that " Jupiter rains not that corn may be increased, but from necessity. Similarly, if some one's corn is destroyed by rain, it does

not rain for this purpose, but as an accidental cir-
cumstance. It does not appear to be from fortune
or chance that it frequently rains in winter, but from
necessity." (3) On the question of the origin of life-
forms he was nearest of all to its modern solution,
setting forth the necessity " that germs should have
been first produced, and not immediately animals;
and that soft mass which first subsisted was the germ.
In plants, also, there is purpose, but it is less distinct;
and this shows that plants were produced in the same
manner as animals, not by chance, as by the union
of olives with grape vines. Similarly, it may be
argued, that there should be an accidental generation of the germs of things, but he who asserts this
subverts Nature herself, for Nature produces those
things which, being continually moved by a certain
principle contained in themselves, arrive at a certain end." In the eagerness of theologians to discover proof of a belief in one God among the old philosophers, the references made by Aristotle to a
" perfecting principle," an " efficient cause," a " prime
mover," and so forth, have been too readily construed
as denoting a monotheistic creed which, reminding
us of the " one god " of Xenophanes, is also akin to
the Personal God of Christianity. " The Stagirite,"
as Mr. Benn remarks (Greek Philosophers, vol. i,
p. 312), " agrees with Catholic theism, and he agrees
with the First Article of the English Church, though
not with the Pentateuch, in saying that God is without parts or passions, but there his agreement ceases.

Excluding such a thing as divine interference with all Nature, his theology, of course, excludes the possibility of revelation, inspiration, miracles, and grace." He is a being who does not interest himself in human affairs.

But, differ as the commentators may as to Aristotle's meaning, his assumed place in the orthodox line led, as will be seen hereafter, to the acceptance of his philosophy by Augustine, Bishop of Hippo, in the fourth century, and by other Fathers of the Church, so that the mediæval theories of the Bible, blended with Aristotle, represent the sum of knowledge held as sufficient until the discoveries of Copernicus in the sixteenth century upset the Ptolemaic theory with its fixed earth and system of cycles and epicycles in which the heavenly bodies moved. He thereby upset very much besides. Like Anaximander and others, Aristotle believed in spontaneous generation, although only in the case of certain animals, as of eels from the mud of ponds, and of insects from putrid matter. However, in this, both Augustine and Thomas Aquinas, and many men of science down to the latter part of the seventeenth century, followed him. For example, Van Helmont, an experimental chemist of that period, gave a recipe for making fleas; and another scholar showed himself on a level with the unlettered rustics of to-day, who believe that eels are produced from horse hairs thrown into a pond.

Of deeper interest, as marking Aristotle's pre-

vision, is his anticipation of what is known as Epi-
genesis, or the theory of the development of the
germ into the adult form among the higher individuals through the union of the fertilizing powers
of the male and female organs. This theory, which
was proved by the researches of Harvey, the dis-
coverer of the circulation of the blood, and is accepted by all biologists to-day, was opposed by Malpighi, an Italian physician, born in 1628, the year
in which Harvey published his great discovery, and
by other prominent men of science down to the last
century. Malpighi and his school contended that
the perfect animal is already " preformed " in the
germ; for example, the hen's egg, before fecunda-
tion, containing an excessively minute, but complete, chick. It therefore followed that in any germ
the germs of all subsequent offspring must be contained, and in the application of this " box-within-
box " theory its defenders even computed the number of human germs concentrated in the ovary of
mother Eve, estimating these at two hundred thousand millions!

When the " preformation " theory was revived by
Bonnet and others in the eighteenth century, Erasmus Darwin, grandfather of Charles Darwin, passed
the following shrewd criticism on it: " Many ingenious philosophers have found so great difficulty
in conceiving the manner of reproduction in animals
that they have supposed all the numerous progeny
to have existed in miniature in the animal originally

created. This idea, besides its being unsupported by any analogy we are acquainted with, ascribes a greater continuity to organized matter than we can readily admit. These embryos . . . must possess a greater degree of minuteness than that which was ascribed to the devils who tempted St. Anthony, of whom twenty thousand were said to have been able to dance a saraband on the point of a needle without the least incommoding each other."

Although no theistic element could be extracted by the theologians of the early Christian Church from the systems of Empedocles and Democritus, thereby securing them a share in the influence exercised by the great Stagirite, they were formative powers in Greek philosophy, and, moreover, have " come by their own" in these latter days. Their chief representative in what is known as the Post-Aristotelian period is Epicurus, who was born at Samos, 342 B. C. As with Zeno, the founder of the Stoic school, his teaching has been perverted, so that his name has become loosely identified with indulgence in gross and sensual living. He saw in pleasure the highest happiness, and therefore advocated the pursuit of pleasure to attain happiness, but he did not thereby mean the pursuit of the unworthy. Rather did he counsel the following after pure, high, and noble aims, whereby alone a man could have peace of mind. It is not hard to see that in the minds of men of low ideals the tendency towards passivity which lurked in such teaching would

aid their sliding into the pursuit of mere animal en-
joyment; hence the gross and limited association of
the term Epicurean. Epicurus accepted the theory
of Leucippus, and applied it all round. The *fainéant*
gods, who dwell serenely indifferent to human affairs, and about whom men should therefore have no
dread; all things, whether dead or living, even the
ideas that enter the mind; are alike composed of
atoms. He also accepted the theory broached by
Empedocles as to the survival of fit and capable
forms after life had arrived at these through the
processes of spontaneous generation and the production of monstrosities. Adopting the physical
speculations of these forerunners, he made them the
vehicle of didactic and ethical philosophies which inspired the production of the wonderful poem of
Lucretius.

Between this great Roman and Epicurus—a period of some two centuries—there is no name of sufficient prominence to warrant attention. The decline
of Greece had culminated in her conquest by the
semi-barbarian Mummius, and in her consequent addition to the provinces of the Roman Empire. What
life lingered in her philosophy within her own borders expired with the loss of freedom, and the work
done by the Pioneers of Evolution in Greece was to
be resumed elsewhere. In the few years of the pre-
Christian period that remained the teaching of Empedocles, and of Epicurus as the mouthpiece of the
atomic theory, was revived by Lucretius in his De

Rerum Natura. Of that remarkable man but little is recorded, and the record is untrustworthy. He was probably born 99 B. C., and died—by his own hand, Jerome says, but of this there is no proof—in his forty-fourth year. It is difficult, taking up his wonderful poem, to resist the temptation to make copious extracts from it, since, even through the vehicle of Mr. Munro's exquisite translation, it is probably little known to the general reader in these evil days of snippety literature. But the temptation must be resisted, save in moderate degree.

With the dignity which his high mission inspires, Lucretius appeals to us in the threefold character of teacher, reformer, and poet. " First, by reason of the greatness of my argument, and because I set the mind free from the close-drawn bonds of superstition; and next because, on so dark a theme, I compose such lucid verse, touching every point with the grace of poesy." As a teacher he expounds the doctrines of Epicurus concerning life and nature; as a reformer he attacks superstition; as a poet he informs both the atomic philosophy and its moral application with harmonious and beautiful verse swayed by a fervour that is akin to religious emotion.

Discussing at the outset various theories of origins, and dismissing these, notably that which asserts that things came from nothing—" for if so, any kind might be born of anything, nothing would require seed," Lucretius proceeds to expound the teaching of Leucippus and other atomists as to the constitu-

tion of things by particles of matter ruled in their
movements by unvarying laws. This theory he
works all round, explaining the processes by which
the atoms unite to carry on the birth, growth, and
decay of things, the variety of which is due to variety
of form of the atoms and to differences in modes
of their combination; the combinations being determined by the affinities or properties of the atoms
themselves, " since it is absolutely decreed what each
thing can and what it cannot do by the conditions of
Nature." Change is the law of the universe; what
is, will perish, but only to reappear in another form.
Death is "the only immortal"; and it is that and
what may follow it which are the chief tormentors
of men. " This terror of the soul, therefore, and this
darkness, must be dispelled, not by the rays of the
sun or the bright shafts of day, but by the outward
aspect and harmonious plan of Nature." Lucretius
explains that the soul, which he places in the centre
of the breast, is also formed of very minute atoms of
heat, wind, calm air, and a finer essence, the pro-
portions of which determine the character of both
men and animals. It dies with the body, in support
of which statement Lucretius advances seventeen
arguments, so determined is he to "deliver those
who through fear of death are all their lifetime subject to bondage."

These themes fill the first three books. In the
fourth he grapples with the mental problems of
sensation and conception, and explains the origin *oi*

3

belief in immortality as due to ghosts and apparitions which appear in dreams. " When sleep has
prostrated the body, for no other reason does the
mind's intelligence wake, except because the very
same images provoke our minds which provoke them
when we are awake, and to such a degree that we
seem without a doubt to perceive him whom life has
left, and death and earth gotten hold of. This Nature constrains to come to pass because all the senses
of the body are then hampered and at rest throughout the limbs, and cannot refute the unreal by real
things."

In the fifth book Lucretius deals with origins—
of the sun, the moon, the earth (which he held to be
flat, denying the existence of the antipodes); of life
and its development; and of civilization. In all this
he excludes design, explaining everything as produced and maintained by natural agents, "the masses,
suddenly brought together, became the rudiments of
earth, sea, and heaven, and the race of living things."
He believed in the successive appearance of plants
and animals, but in their arising separately and directly out of the earth, " under the influence of rain
and the heat of the sun," thus repeating the old
speculations of the emergence of life from slime,
" wherefore the earth with good title has gotten and
keeps the name of mother." He did not adopt Empedocles's theory of the " four roots of all things,"
and he will have none of the monsters—the hippo-
griffs, chimeras, and centaurs—which form a part of

the scheme of that philosopher. These, he says, " have never existed," thus showing himself far in advance of ages when unicorns, dragons, and such-like fabled beasts were seriously believed to exist. In one respect, more discerning than Aristotle, he accepts the doctrine of the survival of the fittest as taught by the sage of Agrigentum. For he argues that since upon " the increase of some Nature set a ban, so that they could not reach the coveted flower of age, nor find food, nor be united in marriage," . . . " many races of living things have died out, and been unable to beget and continue their breed." Lucretius speaks of Empedocles in terms scarcely less exaggerated than those which he applied to Epicurus. The latter is " a god " who first found out that plan of life which is now termed wisdom, and who by tried skill rescued life from such great billows and such thick darkness and moored it in so perfect a calm and in so brilliant a light, . . . he cleared men's breasts with truth-telling precepts, and fixed a limit to lust and fear, and explained what was the chief good which we all strive to reach." As to Empedocles, " that great country (Sicily) seems to have held within it nothing more glorious than this man, nothing more holy, marvellous, and dear. The verses, too, of this godlike genius cry with a loud voice, and make known his great discoveries, so that he seems scarcely born of a mortal stock."

Continuing his speculations on the development of living things, Lucretius strikes out in bolder and

original vein. The past history of man, he says, lies
in no heroic or golden age, but in one of struggle
out of savagery.   Only when " children, by their
coaxing ways, easily broke down the proud temper
of their fathers," did there arise the family ties out
of which the wider social bond has grown, and soft-
ening and civilizing agencies begin their fair offices.
In his battle for food and shelter, " man's first arms
were hands, nails and teeth and stones and boughs
broken off from the forests, and flame and fire, as
soon as they had become known.   Afterward the
force of iron and copper was discovered, and the use
of copper was known before that of iron, as its nature
is easier to work, and it is found in greater quantity.
With copper they would labour the soil of the earth
and stir up the billows of war. . . . Then by slow
steps the sword of iron gained ground and the make
of the copper sickle became a byword, and with iron
they began to plough through the earth's soil, and
the struggles of wavering man were rendered equal."
As to language, " Nature impelled them to utter the
various sounds of the tongue, and use struck out the
names of things."   Thus does Lucretius point the
road along which physical and mental evolution have
since travelled, and make the whole story subordinate to the high purpose of his poem in deliverance
of the beings whose career he thus traces from superstition.   Man " seeing the system of heaven and the
different seasons of the years could not find out by
what causes this was done, and sought refuge in

handing over all things to the gods and supposing
all things to be guided by their nod." Then, in the
sixth and last book, the completion of which would
seem to have been arrested by his death, Lucretius
explains the "law of winds and storms," of earthquakes and volcanic outbursts, which men "foolishly
lay to the charge of the gods," who thereby make
known their anger.

> So, loath to suffer mute,
> We, peopling the void air,
> Make Gods to whom to impute
> The ills we ought to bear;
> With God and Fate to rail at, suffering easily.

And what a motley crowd of gods they were on
whose caprice or indifference he pours his vials of
anger and contempt! The tolerant pantheon of
Rome gave welcome to any foreign deity with respectable credentials; to Cybele, the Great Mother,
imported in the shape of a rough-hewn stone with
pomp and rejoicings from Phrygia 204 B. C.; to Isis,
welcomed from Egypt; to Herakles, Demeter, As-
klepios, and many another god from Greece. But
these were dismissed from a man's thought when the
prayer or sacrifice to them had been offered at the
due season. They had less influence on the Roman's
life than the crowd of native godlings who were
thinly disguised fetiches, and who controlled every
action of the day. For the minor gods survive the
changes in the pantheon of every race. Of the Greek
peasant of to-day Mr. Rennel Rodd testifies, in his

Custom and Lore of Modern Greece, that much as
he would shudder at the accusation of any taint of
paganism, the ruling of the Fates is more immediately real to him than divine omnipotence.   Mr.
Tozer confirms this in his Highlands of Turkey. He
says: " It is rather the minor deities and those associated with man's ordinary life that have escaped
the brunt of the storm, and returned to live in a dim
twilight of popular belief."   In India, Sir Alfred
Lyall tells us that, " even the supreme triad of Hindu
allegory, which represents the almighty powers of
creation, preservation, and destruction, have long
ceased to preside actively over any such corresponding distribution of functions."   Like limited mon-
archs, they reign, but do not govern.   They are
superseded by the ever-increasing crowd of godlings
whose influence is personal and special, as shown by
Mr. Crooke in his instructive Introduction to the
Popular Religion and Folk-lore of Northern India.

The old Roman catalogue of spiritual beings,
abstractions as they were, who guarded life in minute
detail, is a long one.   From the *indigitamenta,* as
such lists are called, we learn that no less than forty-
three were concerned with the actions of a child.
When the farmer asked Mother Earth for a good
harvest, the prayer would not avail unless he also
invoked " the spirit of breaking up the land and the
spirit of ploughing it crosswise; the spirit of furrow-
ing and the spirit of ploughing in the seed; and the
spirit of harrowing; the spirit of weeding and the

spirit of reaping; the spirit of carrying corn to the barn; and the spirit of bringing it out again." The country, moreover, swarmed with Chaldæan astrologers and casters of nativities; with Etruscan haruspices full of " childish lightning-lore," who foretold events from the entrails of sacrificed animals; while in competition with these there was the State-supported college of augurs to divine the will of the gods by the cries and direction of the flight of birds. Well might the satirist of such a time say that the "place was so densely populated with gods as to leave hardly room for the men."

It will be seen that the justification for including Lucretius among the Pioneers of Evolution lies in his two signal and momentous contributions to the science of man; namely, the primitive savagery of the human race, and the origin of the belief in a soul and a future life. Concerning the first, anthropological research, in its vast accumulation of materials during the last sixty years, has done little more than fill in the outline which the insight of Lucretius enabled him to sketch. As to the second, he anticipates, well-nigh in detail, the ghost-theory of the origin of belief in spirits generally which Herbert Spencer and Dr. Tylor, following the lines laid down by Hume and Turgot (see p. 255), have formulated and sustained by an enormous mass of evidence. The credit thus due to Lucretius for the original ideas in his majestic poem—Greek in conception and Roman in execution—has been ob-

scured in the general eclipse which that poem suffered for centuries through its anti-theological spirit.
Grinding at the same philosophical mill, Aristotle,
because of the theism assumed to be involved in his
" perfecting principle," was cited as " a pillar of the
faith " by the Fathers and Schoolmen; while Lucretius, because of his denial of design, was " anathema
maranatha." Only in these days, when the far-reaching effects of the theory of evolution, supported by
observation in every branch of inquiry, are apparent,
are the merits of Lucretius as an original seer, more
than as an expounder of the teachings of Empedocles
and Epicurus, made clear.

Standing well-nigh on the threshold of the Christian era, we may pause to ask what is the sum of
the speculation into the causes and nature of things
which, begun in Ionia (with impulse more or less
slight from the East, in the sixth century before
Christ), by Thales, ceased, for many centuries, in the
poem of Lucretius, thus covering an active period
of about five hundred years. The caution not to see
in these speculations more than an approximate approach to modern theories must be kept in mind.

1. There is a primary substance which abides
amidst the general flux of things.

*All modern research tends to show that the various
combinations of matter are formed of some* prima ma-
teria. *But its ultimate nature remains unknown.*

2. Out of nothing comes nothing.

Modern science knows nothing of a beginning, and, moreover, holds it to be unthinkable. In this it stands in direct opposition to the theological dogma that God created the universe out of nothing; a dogma still accepted by the majority of Protestants and binding on Roman Catholics. For the doctrine of the Church of Rome thereon, as expressed in the Canons of the Vatican Council, is as follows: " If any one confesses not that the world and all things which are contained in it, both spiritual and mental, have been, in their whole substance, produced by God out of nothing; or shall say that God created, not by His free will from all necessity, but by a necessity equal to the necessity whereby He loves Himself, or shall deny that the world was made for the glory of God: let him be anathema."

3. The primary substance is indestructible.

The modern doctrine of the Conservation of Energy teaches that both matter and motion can neither be created nor destroyed.

4. The universe is made up of indivisible particles called atoms, whose manifold combinations, ruled by unalterable affinities, result in the variety of things.

With modifications based on chemical as well as mechanical changes among the atoms, this theory of Leucippus and Democritus is confirmed. (But recent experiments and discoveries show that reconstruction of chemical theories as to the properties of the atom may happen.)

5. Change is the law of things, and is brought about by the play of opposing forces.

Modern science explains the changes in phenomena as due to the antagonism of repelling and attracting modes of motion; when the latter overcome the former, equilibrium will be reached, and the present state of things will come to an end.

6. Water is a necessary condition of life.

Therefore life had its beginnings in water; a theory wholly indorsed by modern biology.

7. Life arose out of non-living matter.

Although modern biology leaves the origin of life as an insoluble problem, it supports the theory of fundamental continuity between the inorganic and the organic.

8. Plants came before animals: the higher organisms are of separate sex, and appeared subsequent to the lower.

Generally confirmed by modern biology, but with qualification as to the undefined borderland between the lowest plants and the lowest animals. And, of course, it recognises a continuity in the order and succession of life which was not grasped by the Greeks. Aristotle and others before him believed that some of the higher forms sprang from slimy matter direct.

9. Adverse conditions cause the extinction of some organisms, thus leaving room for those better fitted.

Herein lay the crude germ of the modern doctrine of the " survival of the fittest."

10. Man was the last to appear, and his primitive state was one of savagery. His first tools and weapons were of stone; then, after the discovery of metals, of copper; and, following that, of iron. His body and soul are alike compounded of atoms, and the soul is extinguished at death.

The science of Prehistoric Archæology confirms the theory of man's slow passage from barbarism to civilization; and the science of Comparative Psychology declares that the evidence of his immortality is neither stronger nor weaker than the evidence of the immortality of the lower animals.

Such, in very broad outline, is the legacy of suggestive theories bequeathed by the Ionian school and its successors, theories which fell into the rear when Athens became a centre of intellectual life in which discussion passed from the physical to those ethical problems which lie outside the range of this survey. Although Aristotle, by his prolonged and careful observations, forms a conspicuous exception, the fact abides that insight, rather than experiment, ruled Greek speculation, the fantastic guesses of parts of which themselves evidence the survival of the crude and false ideas about earth and sky long prevailing. The more wonderful is it, therefore, that so much therein points the way along which inquiry travelled after its subsequent long arrest; and the more apparent is it that nothing in science or art, and but little in theological speculations, at least among us

Westerns, can be understood without reference to Greece.

TABLE.

Name.	Place.	Approximate date B. C.	Speciality.
Thales.	Miletus (Ionia).	600	Cosmological Theory as to the Primary Substance } Water.
Anaximender.	"	570	" the Boundless.
Anaximenes.	"	500	" Air.
Pythagoras.	Samos (near the Ionian coast).	500	" Numbers: "a Cosmos built up of geometrical figures," or (Grote, Plato, i, 12) "generated out of number."
Xenophanes.	Colophon (Ionia).	500	Founder of the Eleatic school.
Heraclitus.	Ephesus (Ionia).	500	" Fire.
Empedocles.	Agrigentum (Sicily).	450	" Fire, Air, Earth, and Water: ruled by Love and Strife.
Anaxagoras.	Clazomenae (Ionia).	450	" Nous.
Leucippus Democritus.	Abdera (Thrace).	460	Formulators of the Atomic Theory.
Aristotle.	Stagira (Macedonia).	350	Naturalist.
Epicurus.	Samos.	300	Expounder of the Atomic Theory and Ethical Philosopher.
Lucretius.	Rome.	50	Interpreter of Epicurus and Empedocles: the first Anthropologist.

PART II.

THE ARREST OF INQUIRY.

A. D. 50–A. D. 400.

1. *From the Early Christian Period to the Time of Augustine.*

" A revealed dogma is always opposed to the free research that may
contradict it. The result of science is not to banish the divine
altogether, but ever to place it at a greater distance from the
world of particular facts in which men once believed they saw
it."—RENAN, Essay on Islamism and Science.

A DETAILED account of the rise and progress of
the Christian religion is not within the scope of this
book. But as that religion, more especially in the
elaborated theological form which it ultimately assumed, became the chief barrier to the development
of Greek ideas; except, as has been remarked, in
the degree that these were represented by Aristotle,
and brought into harmony with it; a short survey
of its origin and early stages is necessary to the continuity of our story.

The history of that great movement is told according to the bias of the writers. They explain
its rapid diffusion and its ultimate triumph over
Paganism as due either to its Divine origin and
guidance; or to the favourable conditions of the time
of its early propagation, and to that wise adaptation
to circumstances which linked its fortunes with those

37

of the progressive peoples of Western Europe. In the judgment of every unofficial narrator, this latter explanation best accords with the facts of history, and with the natural causes which largely determine success or failure. The most partisan advocates of its supernatural, and therefore special, character have to show reason why the fortunes of the Christian religion have varied like those of other great religions, both older and younger than it; why, like Buddhism, it has been ousted from the country in which it rose; and why, in competition with Brahmanism, as Sir Alfred Lyall testifies in his Asiatic Studies (p. 110), and with Mohammedanism in Africa, it has less success than these in the mission fields where it comes into rivalry with them. Riven into wrangling sects from an early period of its history, it has, while exercising a beneficent influence in turbulent and lawless ages, brought not " peace on earth, but a sword." It has been the cause of undying hate, of bloody wars, and of persecutions between parties and nations, whose animosity seems the deeper when stirred by matters which are incapable of proof. As Montaigne says, " Nothing is so firmly believed as that which is least known." To bring the Christian religion, or, rather, its manifold forms, from the purest spiritualistic to such degraded type as exists, for example, in Abyssinia, within the operation of the law which governs development, and which, therefore, includes partial and local corruption; is to make its history as clear as it is pro-

THE ARREST OF INQUIRY.

foundly instructive; while, to demand for it an origin and character different in kind from other religions, is to import confusion into the story of mankind, and to raise a swarm of artificial difficulties. " If," as John Morley observes in his criticism of Turgot's dissertation upon The Advantages that the Establishment of Christianity has conferred upon the Human Race (Miscell., vol. ii, p. 90), " there had been in the Christian idea the mysterious self-sowing quality so constantly claimed for it, how came it that in the Eastern part of the Empire it was as powerless for spiritual or moral regeneration as it was for political health and vitality; while in the Western part it became the organ of the most important of all the past transformations of the civilized world? Is not the difference to be explained by the difference in the surrounding medium, and what is the effect of such an explanation upon the supernatural claims of the Christian idea?" Its inclusion as one of other modes, varying only in degree, by which man has progressed from the " ape and tiger " stage to the highest ideals of the race, makes clear what concerns us here, namely, its attitude toward secular knowledge, and the consequent serious arrest of that knowledge. That a religion which its followers claim to be of supernatural origin, and secured from error by the perpetual guidance of a Holy Spirit, should have opposed inquiry into matters the faculty for investigating which lay within human power and province; that it should actually have put to death those who dared thus to inquire, and to make known what they had discovered; is a problem which its advocates may settle among themselves. It is no problem to those who take the opposite view.

In outlining the history of Christianity stress will be here laid only upon those elements which caused it to be an arresting force in man's intellectual development, and, therefore, in his spiritual emancipation from terrors begotten of ignorance. It does not fall within our survey to speak of that primary element in it which was before all dogma, and which may survive when dogma has become only a matter of antiquarian interest. That element, born of emotion, which, as a crowd of kindred examples show, incarnates, and then deifies the object of its worship, was the belief in the manifestation of the divine through the human Jesus who had borne men's griefs, carried their sorrows, and offered rest to the weary and heavy-laden. For no religion—and here Evolution comes in as witness—can take root which does not adapt itself to, and answer some need of, the heart of man. Hence the importance of study of the history of all religions.

Evolution knows only one heresy—the denial of continuity. Recognising the present as the outcome of the past, it searches after origins. It knows that both that which revolts us in man's spiritual history has, alike with that which attracts, its place, its necessary place, in the development of ideas, and is, therefore, capable of explanation from its roots upward. For this age is sympathetic, not flippant. It looks with no favour on criticism that is only destructive, or on ridicule or ribaldry as modes of attack on current beliefs. Hence we have the modern science of comparative theology, with its Hibbert Lectures, and Gifford Lectures, which are critical and constructive; as opposed to Bampton Lectures, Boyle and Hulse Lectures, which are apologetic, the speaker holding an official brief. Of the Boyle Lecturers, Collings the " Deist" caustically said that nobody doubted the existence of the Deity till they set to work to prove it. Religions are no longer treated as true or false, as inventions of priests or of divine origin, but as the product of man's intellectual speculations, however crude or coarse; and of his spiritual needs, no matter in what repulsive form they are satisfied. For " proofs " and " evidences " we have substituted explanations.

Nevertheless, so strong, often so bitter, are the feelings aroused over the most temperate discussion of the origin of Christianity that it remains necessary to repeat that to explain is not to attack, and that to narrate is not to apportion blame, for no religion can do aught than reflect the temper of the age in which it flourishes.

Let us now summarize certain occurrences which, although familiar enough, must be repeated for the clear understanding of their effects.

Some sixty years after the death of Lucretius

4

there happened, in the subsequent belief of millions of mankind, an event for which all that had gone before in the history of this planet is said to have been a preparation. In the fulness of time the Omnipotent maker and ruler of a universe to which no boundaries can be set by human thought, sent to this earth-speck no less a person than His Eternal Son. He was said to have been born, not by the natural processes of generation, but to have been incarnated in the womb of a virgin, retaining his divine nature while subjecting it to human limitations. This he had done that he might, as sinless man, become an expiatory sacrifice to offended deity, and to the requirements of divine justice, for the sins which the human race had committed since the transgression of Adam and Eve, or which men yet to be born might commit.

The " miraculous " birth of Jesus took place at Nazareth in Galilee, in the reign of Cæsar Augustus, about 750 A. U. C., as the Romans reckoned time. Tradition afterward fixed his birthday on the 25th December, which, curiously enough, although, perhaps, explaining the choice, was the day dedicated to the sun-god Mithra, an Oriental deity to whom altars had been raised and sacrifices performed, with rites of baptisms of blood, in hospitable Rome.

Jesus is said to have lived in the obscurity of his native mountain village till his thirtieth year. Except one doubtful story of his going to Jerusalem with his parents when he was twelve years old, noth-

ing is recorded in the various biographies of him
between his birth and his appearance as a public
teacher. Probably he followed his father's trade as
a carpenter. The event that seems to have called
him from home was the preaching of an enthusiastic ascetic named John the Baptist. At his hands
Jesus submitted to the baptismal rite, and then entered on his career, wandering from place to place.
The fragments of his discourses, which have survived
in the short biographies known as the Gospels, show
him to have been gifted with a simple, winning style,
and his sermons, brightened by happy illustration
or striking parable, went home to the hearts of his
hearers. Women, often of the outcast class, were
drawn to him by the sympathy which attracted even
more than his teaching. Among a people to whom
the unvarying order of Nature was an idea wholly
foreign—for Greek speculations had not penetrated
into Palestine—stories of miracle-working found
easy credit, falling in, as they did, with popular belief in the constant intervention of deity. Thus, to
the reports of what Jesus taught were added those
of the wonders which he had wrought, from feeding
thousands of folk with a few loaves of bread to rais-
ing the dead to life. His itinerant mission secured
him a few devoted followers from various towns and
villages, while the effect of success upon himself
was to heighten his own conception of the importance of his work. The skill of the Romans in fusing
together subject races had failed them in the case of

the Jews, whose belief in their special place in the world as the "chosen people" never forsook them. Nor had their misfortunes weakened their belief that the Messiah predicted by their prophets would appear to deliver them, and plant their feet on the neck of the hated conqueror. This hope, as became a pious Jew, Jesus shared, but it set him brooding on some nobler, because more spiritual, conception of it than his fellow-countrymen nurtured. Finally, it led him to the belief, fostered by the ambition of his nearer disciples, which was, however, material in its hopes, that he was the spiritual Messiah. In that faith he repaired to Jerusalem at the time of the Passover feast when the city was crowded with devotees, that he might, before the chief priests and elders, make his appeal to the nation. According to the story, his daring in clearing the holy temple of money-changers and traders led to his appearance before the Sanhedrin, the highest judicial council; his plainness of speech raised the fury of the sects; and when, dreaming of a purer faith, he spoke ominous words about the destruction of the temple, the charge of blasphemy was laid against him. His guilt was made clear to his judges when, answering a question of the high priest, he declared himself to be the Messiah. This, involving claim to kingship over the Jews, and therefore rebellion against the Empire, was made the plea of haling him before the Roman governor, Pontius Pilate, for trial. Pilate, looking upon the whole affair as a local *émeute*, was disin-

clined to severity, but nothing short of the death of
Jesus as a blasphemer (although his chief offence
appears to have been his disclaimer of earthly sov-
ereignty) would satisfy the angry mob. Amidst their
taunts and jeers he was taken to a place named Cal-
vary, and there put to death by the torturing process
of crucifixion, or, the particular mode not being clear,
of transfixion on a stake.

This tragic event, on which, as is still widely held,
hang the destinies of mankind to the end of time,
attracted no attention outside Judæa. In the
Roman eye, cold, contemptuous, and practical, it was
but the execution of a troublesome fanatic who had
embroiled himself with his fellow-countrymen, and
added the crime of sedition to the folly of blasphemy.
Pilate himself passed on, without more ado, to the
next duty. Tradition, anxious to prove that retri-
bution followed his criminal act, as it was judged in
after-time to be, tells how he flung himself in remorse
from the mountain known as Pilatus, which overlooks the lake of Lucerne. With truer insight, a
striking modern story, L'Etui de Nacre, by Anatole
France, makes Pilate, on his retirement to Sicily in
old age, thus refer to the incident in conversation
with a Roman friend who had loved a Jewish maiden.

"A few months after I had lost sight of her I heard by
accident that she had joined a small party of men and women
who were following a young Galilean miracle-worker. His
name was Jesus, he came from Nazareth, and he was crucified
for I don't know what crime. Pontius, do you remember this
man? Pontius Pilate knit his brow, and put his hand to his

forehead like one who is searching his memory; then after a
few moments of silence: 'Jesus,' murmured he, 'Jesus of
Nazareth. No, I don't remember him.'"

On the third day after his death, Jesus is said to
have risen from the grave, and appeared to a faithful few of his disciples. On the fortieth day after
his resurrection he is said to have ascended to heaven.
Both these statements rest on the authority of the
biographies which were compiled some years after
his death. Jesus wrote nothing himself; therefore
the "brethren," as his intimate followers called one
another, had no other sacred books than those of the
Old Testament. They believed that Jesus was the
Messiah predicted in Daniel and some of the apocry-
phal writings, and they cherished certain "logia" or
sayings of his which formed the basis of the first
three Gospels. The earliest of these, that bearing
the name of Mark, probably took the shape in which
we have it (some spurious verses at the end excepted)
about 70 A. D. The fourth Gospel, which tradition
attributes to John, is generally believed to be half a
century later than Mark. It seems likely that the
importance of collecting the words of Jesus into any
permanent form did not occur to those who had
heard them, because the belief in his speedy return
was all-powerful among them, and their life and attitude toward everything was shaped accordingly.

Without sacred books, priesthood, or organization, these earliest disciples, whom the fate of their
leader had driven into hiding for a time, gathered

themselves into groups for communion and worship.
" In the church of Jerusalem," says Selden in his
Table Talk (xiv), " the Christians were but another
sect of Jews that did believe the Messias was come."
From that sacred city there went forth preachers of
this simple doctrine through the lands where Greek-
speaking Jews, known as those of the Dispersion,
had been long settled. These formed a very important element in the Roman Empire, being scattered
from Asia Minor to Egypt, and thence in all the
lands washed by the Mediterranean. As their racial
isolation and national hopes made them the least
contented among the subject-peoples, a series of tolerant measures securing them certain privileges, subject to loyal behaviour, had been prudently granted
by their Roman masters. The new teaching spread
from Antioch to Alexandria and Rome. But early
in the onward career of the movement a division
broke out among the immediate disciples of Jesus
which ended in lasting rupture. A distinguished
convert had been won to the faith in the person of
the Apostle Paul. He is the real founder of Christianity as a more or less systematized creed, and all
the development of dogma which followed are integral parts of the structure raised by him. He converted it from a local religion into a widespread
faith. This came about, at the start, through his defeat of the narrower section headed by Peter, who
would have compelled all non-Jewish converts to
submit to the rite of circumcision.

The unity of the Empire gave Christianity its chance. Through the connection of Eurasia from the Euphrates to the Atlantic by magnificent roads, communication between peoples followed the lines of least resistance. Happily for the future of Christianity, the early missionaries travelled westward, in the wake of the dispersed Jews, along the Mediterranean seaboard, and thus its fortunes became identified with the civilizing portion of mankind. Had they travelled eastward, it might have been blended with Buddhism, or, as its Gnostic phases show, become merged in Oriental mysticism. The story of progress ran smoothly till A. D. 64, when we first hear of the " Christians "—for by such name they had become known—in " profane " history, as it was once oddly called. Tacitus, writing many years after the event, tells how on the night of the 18th July, in the sixty-fourth year of our era, a fierce fire broke out in Rome, causing the destruction of magnificent buildings raised by Augustus, and of priceless works of Greek art. Suspicion fell on Nero, and he, as has been suggested, was instigated by his wife Poppaea Sabina, an unscrupulous woman, and, according to some authorities, a convert to Judaism, " to put an end to the common talk, by imputing the fire to others, visiting, with a refinement of punishment, those detestable criminals who went by the name of Christians. The author of that denomination was Christus, who had been executed in the time of Tiberius, by the procurator, Pontius

Pilate." Tacitus goes on to describe Christianity as " a pestilent superstition," and its adherents as guilty of " hatred to the human race." The indictment, on the face of it, seems strange, but it has an explanation, although the Christians were brutally murdered on the charge of arson, and not of superstition. So far as religious persecution went, they suffered this first at the hands of Jews, the Empire intervening to protect them. Broadly speaking, the Roman note was toleration. Throughout the Empire religion was a national affair, because it began and ended with the preservation of the State. Thereupon it was the binding duty—*religio*—of every citizen to pay due honour to the protecting gods on whose favour the safety of the State depended. That done, a man might believe what he chose. Polytheism is, from its nature, easy-going and tolerant; so long as there was no open opposition to the authorized public worship, the worshipper could explain it any way he chose. In Greece a man " might believe or disbelieve that the Mysteries taught the doctrine of immortality; the essential thing was that he should duly sacrifice his pig." In Rome, that vast Cosmopolis, " the ordinary pagan did not care two straws whether his neighbour worshipped twenty gods or twenty-one." Why should he care?

Now, against all this, the Christians set their faces sternly, and the result was to make them regarded as anti-patriotic and anti-social. Their success among the lower classes had been rapid. Chris-

tianity levelled all distinctions: it welcomed the master and his slave, the outcast and the pure: it treated
woman as the spiritual equal of man: it held out to
each the hope of a future life.   Thus far, all was to
the good, although the old Mithraic religion had
done well-nigh as much.   But Christianity held aloof
from the common social life, putting itself out of
touch with the manifold activity of Rome.   It sought
to apply certain maxims of Jesus literally; it dis-
couraged marriage, it brought disunion into family
life; it counselled avoidance of service in the army
or acceptance of any public office.   This general
attitude was wholly due to the belief that with the
return of Jesus, the end of the world was at hand.
For Jesus had foretold his second coming, and the
earliest epistles of the apostles bade the faithful prepare for it.   Here there was no continuing city; citi-
zenship was in heaven, for the kingdom of Christ
was not of this world.   Therefore to give thought to
the earthly and fleeting was folly and impiety, for
who would care to heap up wealth, to strive for place
or to pursue pleasure, or to search after what men
called "wisdom," when these imperilled the soul,
and blocked the way to heaven?

The prejudice created by this belief, expressed in
such direct action as refusal to worship the guardian
gods and the "genius" of the Emperor, was deep-
ened by ugly, although baseless, rumours as to the
cruel and immoral things done by the Christians at
their secret meetings.   And so it came to pass that

Tacitus spoke of Christianity in the terms quoted; that Epictetus and Marcus Aurelius (who refers to it only once in his Meditations) dismissed it with a scornful phrase; that the common people called it atheistic; and that, finally, it became a proscribed and persecuted religion.

Further than this there is no need to pursue its career until, with wholly changed fortunes, we meet it as a tolerated religion under a so-called Christian Emperor. The object in tracing it thus far is to indicate how enthusiasts, thus filled with an anti-worldly spirit, would become and remain an arresting force against the advance of inquiry and, therefore, of knowledge; and how, as their religion gathered power, and itself became worldly in policy, it would the more strongly assert supremacy over the reason. For intellectual activity would lead to inquiry into the claims and authority of the Church, and inquiry, therefore, was the thing to be proscribed. Then, too, the committal of the floating biographies of Jesus to written form, and their grouping, with the letters of the apostles, into one more or less complete collection, to be afterward called the New Testament (a collection held to embrace, as the theory of inspiration became formulated, all that it is needful for man to know), would create a further barrier against intellectual activity. Then, as Christianity came into nearer touch with the enfeebled remnants of Greek philosophy, and with other foreign influences shaping its dogmas, discussions about

the person of Christ became active. The simple flu-
ent creed of the early Christians took rigid form in
the subtleties of the Nicene Creed, and as " Very
God of Very God " the final appeal was, logically, to
the words of Jesus. Hence another barrier against
inquiry.

Conflict has never arisen on the ethical sayings
of Jesus, which, making allowance for the impracti-
cableness of a few, place him high among the sages
of antiquity. Comparing their teaching with his, it
is easy to group together maxims which do not yield
to the more famous examples in the Sermon on the
Mount as guides to conduct, or as inspiration to
high ideals. The " golden rule " is anticipated by
Plato's " Thou shalt not take that which is mine,
and may I do to others as I would that they should
do to me " (Jowett's translation, v, p. 483). And
it is paralleled by Isocrates, a contemporary of Plato,
in those words spoken by the King Nicocles when
addressing his governors, " You should be to others
what you think I should be to you." But if there was
nothing new in what Jesus taught, there was fresh-
ness in the method. Conflict is waged only over
statements the nature and limits of which might be
expected from the place and age when they were
delivered. They who hold that Jesus was God the
Son Eternal, and therefore incapable of error, may
reconcile, as best they can with this, his belief in the
mischievous delusions of his time. If they say that
so much of this as may be reported in the records of

his life are spurious, they throw the whole contents
of the gospels into the melting-pot of criticism.

Taking the narratives as we have them, documents stamped with the hall-mark of the centuries,
" declaring," as a body of clergymen proclaimed recently, " incontrovertibly the actual historical truth
in all records, both of past events, and of the delivery of predictions to be thereafter fulfilled," we learn
that Jesus accepted the accuracy of the sacred writings of his people; that he spoke of Moses as the
author of the Pentateuch; that he referred to its legends as dealing with historical persons, and as re-
porting actual events. All these beliefs are refuted
by the critical scholarship of to-day. We need not
go to Germany for the verdict; it is indorsed by
eminent Hebraists, officials of the Church of England. Canon Driver, Professor of Hebrew at Oxford, says that " like other people, the Jews formed
theories to account for the beginnings of the earth
and man "; that " they either did this for themselves,
or borrowed from their neighbours," and that " of
the theories current in Assyria and Phoenicia fragments have been preserved which exhibit parts of
resemblance to the Bible narratives sufficient to warrant the inference that both are derived from the
same cycle of traditions." If, therefore, the cosmogonic and other legends are inspired, so must also
the common original of these and their corresponding stories be inspired. The matter might be pur-
sued through the patriarchal age to the eve of the

Exodus, showing that, here also, the mythical element is dominant; the existence of Abraham himself dissolving in the solution of the " higher criticism." As to the Pentateuch, the larger number of scholars place its composition, in the form in which we have it—older documents being blended therein —about the sixth and fifth centuries B. C.

Jesus spoke of the earth as if it were flat, and the most important among the heavenly bodies. Knowledge of the active speculations that went on centuries before his time on the Ionian seaboard; prevision of what secrets men would wrest from the stars centuries hence—of neither did he dream. That Homer and Virgil had sung; that Plato had discoursed; that Buddha had founded a religion with which his, when Western activity met Eastern passivity, would vainly compete; these, and aught else that had moved the great world without, were unknown to the Syrian teacher.

Jesus believed in an arch-fiend, who was permitted by Omnipotence, the Omnipotence against which he had rebelled, to set loose countless numbers of evil spirits to work havoc on men and animals. Jesus also believed in a hell of eternal torment for the wicked; and in a heaven of unending happiness for the good. There is no surer index of the intellectual stage of any people than the degree in which belief in the supernatural, and especially in the activity of supernatural agents, rules their lives. The lower we descend, the more detailed and famil-

iar is the assumption of knowledge of the behaviour
of these agents, and of the nature of the places they
come from or haunt. Of this, mediæval speculations
on demonology, and modern books of anthropology,
supply any number of examples. Here we are concerned only with the momentous fact that belief in
demoniacal activity pervades the New Testament
from beginning to end, and, therefore, gave the warrant for the unspeakable cruelties with which that
belief has stained the annals of Christendom. John
Wesley was consistent when he wrote that " Giving
up the belief in witchcraft was in effect giving up
the Bible," and it may be added that giving up belief in the devil is giving up belief in the atonement
—the central doctrine of the Christian faith. To this
the early Christians would have subscribed: so, also,
would the great Augustine, who said that " nothing
is to be accepted save on the authority of Scripture,
since greater is that authority than all the powers
of the human mind "; so would all who have followed
him in ancient confessions of the faith. It is only
the amorphous form of that faith which, lingering
on, anæmic and boneless, denies by evasion.

But they who abandon belief in maleficent demons and in witches; as also, for this follows, in beneficent agents, as angels; land themselves in serious
dilemma. For to this are such committed. If Jesus,
who came " that he might destroy the works of the
devil," and who is reported, among other proofs of
his divine ministry, to have cast out demons from

" possessed " human beings, and, in one case, to have permitted a crowd of the infernal agents to enter into a herd of swine; if he verily believed that he actually did these things; and if it be true that the belief is a superstition limited to the ignorant or barbaric mind; *what value can be attached to any statement that Jesus is reported to have made about a spiritual world?*

Here then (1) in the attitude of the early Christians toward all mundane affairs as of no moment compared with those affecting their souls' salvation; (2) in the assumed authority of Scripture as a full revelation of both earthly and heavenly things; and (3) in the assumed infallibility of the words of Jesus reported therein; we have three factors which suffice to explain why the great movement toward discovery of the orderly relations of phenomena was arrested for centuries, and theories of capricious government of the universe sheltered and upheld.

While, as has been said, the unity of the Empire secured Christianity its fortunate start; the multiform elements of which the Empire was made up— philosophic and pagan—being gradually absorbed by Christianity, secured it acceptance among the different subject-peoples. The break up of the Empire secured its supremacy.

The absorption of foreign ideas and practices by Christianity, largely through the influence of Hellenic Jews, was an added cause of arrest of inquiry. The adoption of pagan rites and customs, resting, as these did, on a bedrock of barbarism, dragged it to a lower level. The intrusion of philosophic subtleties led to terms being mistaken for explanations: as Gibbon says, "the pride of the professors and of their disciples was satisfied with the science of words." The inchoate and mobile character of Christianity during the first three centuries gave both influences—pagan and philosophic—their opportunity. For long years the converts scattered throughout the Empire were linked together, in more or less regular federation, by the acknowledgment of Christ as Lord, and by the expectation of his second coming. There was no official priesthood, only overseers—"episkopoi"—for social purposes, who made no claims to apostolic succession; no formulated set of doctrines; no Apostles' Creed; no dogmas of baptismal regeneration or of the real presence; no worship or apotheosis of Mary as the Mother of God; no worship of saints or relics.

On the philosophic side, it was the Greek influence in the person of the more educated converts that shaped the dogmas of the Church and sought to blend them with the occult and mysterious elements in Oriental systems, of which modern "Theosophy" is the tenuous parody. That old Greek habit of asking questions, of seeking to reach the reason of things, which, as has been seen, gave the great impulse to scientific inquiry, was as active as ever. Appeals to the Old Testament touched not the Greek as they did the Jewish Christian, and the Canon of

5

the New Testament was as yet unsettled. Strange as it may seem in view of the assumed divine origin of the Gospels and Epistles, human judgment took upon itself to decide which of them were, and which were not, an integral part of supernatural revelation. The ultimate verdict, so far as the Western Church was concerned, was delivered by the Council of Carthage in the early part of the fifth century. There arose a school of Apologists, founders of theology, who, to quote Gibbon, " equipped the Christian religion for the conquest of the Roman world by changing it into a philosophy, attested by Revelation. They mingled together the metaphysics of Platonism, the doctrine of the Logos, which came from the Stoics, morality partly Platonic, partly Stoic, methods of argument and interpretation learnt from Philo, with the pregnant maxims of Jesus and the religious language of the Christian congregations." Thus the road was opened for additions to dogmatic theology, doctrines of the Trinity, of the Virgin Birth, and whatever else could be inferentially extracted from the Scriptures, and blended with foreign ideas. The growing complexity of creed called for interpretation of it, and this obviously fell to the overseers or bishops, chosen for their special gifts of " the grace of the truth." These met, as occasion required, to discuss subjects affecting the faith and discipline of the several groups. Among such, precedence, as a matter of course, would be accorded to the overseer of the most important Christian society in the Empire; and hence the prominence and authority, from an early period, of the bishop of Rome. In the simple and business-like act of his election as chairman of the gatherings lay the germ of the audacious and preposterous claims of the Papacy.

On the pagan side, the course of development is not so easily traced. To determine when and where this or that custom or rite arose is now impossible; indeed, we may say, without exaggeration, that it never arose at all, because the conditions for its adoption were present throughout in human tendencies. The first Christian disciples were Jews: and the ritual which they followed was the direct outcome of ideas common to all barbaric religions, so that certain of the pagan rites and ceremonies with which they came in contact in all parts of the Empire fitted in with custom, tradition, and desire. And this applies, with stronger force, to the converts scattered from Edessa, east of the Euphrates, to the Empire's westernmost limits in Britain. Moreover, we know that a policy of adaptation and conciliation wisely governed the ruling minds of the Church, in whom, stripped of all the verbiage about them as semi-inspired successors of the apostles, there was deep-seated superstition. Paganism might, in its turn, be suppressed by Imperial edict, but it had too much in common with the later forms of Christianity not to survive in fact, however changed in name.

It may be taken as a truism that in the ceremonies of the higher religions there are no inven-

tions, only survivals. This fact sent thinkers like
Hobbes, and dealers in literary antiquities of the type
of Burton, Bishop Newton, and, notablest of all,
Conyers Middleton, on the search after parallels,
which have received astonishing confirmation in our
day. Burton sees the mimicry of the " arch-deceiver
in the strange sacraments, the priests, and the sacrifices," as the Romanist missionaries to Tibet saw
the same diabolical parody of their rites in Buddhist
temples. But Hobbes, with the sagacity which might
be expected of him, recognises the continuity of
ideas: " *mutato nomine tantum;* Venus and Cupid
(Hobbes might have added Isis and Horus) appearing as 'the Virgin Mary and her Sonne,' and the
Ἀποθέωσις of the Heathen surviving in the Canonization of Saints. The carrying of the Popes ' by
Switzers under a Canopie' is a ' Relique of the Divine Honours given to Cæsar'; the carriage of
Images in *Procession* 'a Relique of the Greeks and
Romans.' . . . 'The Heathen had also their *Aqua
Lustralis*, that is to say, *Holy Water.* The Church
of Rome imitates them also in their *Holy Dayes.*
They had their *Bacchanalia*, and we have our *Wakes*
answering to them; They their *Saturnalia*, and we
our Carnevalls and Shrove-tuesdays liberty of Serv-
ants; They their Procession of Priapus, we our
fetching-in, erection, and dancing about *May-Poles;*
and Dancing is one kind of worship; They had their
Procession called *Ambarvalia*, and we our Procession
about the Fields in the *Rogation week.*' "

Middleton examined the matter on the spot, and
in his celebrated Letter from Rome gives numerous
examples of "an exact CONFORMITY between POPERY
and PAGANISM." Since few read his book now-a-
days, some of these may be cited, because their presence goes far to explain why the conglomerate religion which Christianity had become was proof
against ideas spurned alike by pagans and ecclesiastics. Visiting the place for classical study, and " not
to notice the fopperies and ridiculous ceremonies of
the present Religion," Middleton soon found himself
" still in old Heathen Rome," with its rituals of primitive Paganism, as if handed down by an uninter-
rupted succession from the priests of old to the
priests of new Rome. The " smoak of the incense "
in the churches transports him to the temple of the
Paphian Venus described by Virgil (Æneid, I, 420);
the surpliced boy waiting on the priest with the thuri-
ble reminds him of sculptures on ancient bas-reliefs
representing heathen sacrifice, with a white-clad attendant on a priest holding a little chest or box in
his hand. The use of holy water suggests numerous parallels. At the entrance to Pagan temples
stood vases of holy liquid, a mixture of salt and
common water; and, on bas-reliefs, the aspergillum
or brush for the ceremony of sprinkling is carved.
In the annual festival of the benediction of horses,
when the animals were sent to the convent of St.
Anthony to be sprinkled (Middleton had his own
horses thus blest " for about eighteenpence of our

money ") there is the survival of a ceremony in the
Circensian games. In the lamps and wax candles
before the shrines of the Madonna and Saints he is
reminded of a passage in Herodotus as to the use of
lights in the Egyptian temples, while we know that
lamps to the Madonna took the place of those before
the images of the Lares, whose chapels stood at the
corners of the streets. The Synod of Elviri (305 A. D.)
forbade the lighting of wax candles during the day
in cemeteries lest the spirits of the saints should be
disquieted, but the custom was too deeply rooted
to be abolished. As for votive offerings, Middleton
truly says that " no one *custom of antiquity* is so frequently mentioned by all their writers " . . . " but
the most common of all *offerings* were *pictures* representing the history of the miraculous cure or deliverance vouchsafed upon the vow of the donor." Of
which offerings, the *blessed Virgin* is so sure always
to carry off the greatest share, that it may be truly
said of her what *Juvenal* says of the *Goddess Isis*,
whose religion was at that time in the greatest vogue in
Rome, that the *painters got their livelihood out of her.*"
Middleton tells the story from Cicero which, not
without covert sympathy, Montaigne quotes in his
Essay on Prognostications. Diagoras, surnamed
the Atheist, being found one day in a temple, was
thus addressed by a friend: " You, who think the
gods take no care of human affairs, do not you see
here by this number of pictures how many people,
for the sake of their vows, have been saved in

storms at sea, and got safe into harbour?" "Yes,"
answered Diagoras, "I see how it is; for those are
never painted who happen to be drowned." There
is nothing new under the sun. Horace (Odes, Bk.
I, v) tells of the shipwrecked sailor who hung up
his clothes as a thank-offering in the temple of the
sea-god who had preserved him; Polydorus Ver-
gilius, who lived in the early part of the sixteenth
century, that is, some 1,500 years after Horace, describes the classic custom of *ex voto* offerings at
length, while Pennant the antiquary, describing the
well of Saint Winifred in Flintshire in the last century, tells of the votive offerings, in the shape of
crutches and other objects, which were hung about
it. To this day the store is receiving additions. The
sick crowd thither as of old they crowded into the
temples of Æsculapius and Serapis; mothers bring
their sick children as in Imperial Rome they took
them to the Temple of Romulus and Remus. A
draught of water from the basin near the bath, or
a plunge in the bath itself, is followed by prayers at
the altar of the chapel which incloses the well. When
the saint's feast-day is held, the afflicted gather to
kiss the reliquary that holds her bones. Perhaps
one of the most pathetic sights in Catholic churches,
especially in out-of-the-way villages, is the altars on
which are hung votive offerings, rude daubs depict-
ing the disease or danger from which the worshipper
has been delivered.

As to the images, tricked out in curious robes

and gewgaws, Middleton " could not help recollect-
ing the picture which old Homer draws of *Q. Hecuba
of Troy*, prostrating herself before the *miraculous
Image of Pallas*," while his wonder at the Loretto
image of the " Queen of Heaven " with " a face as
black as a Negus " reminds him of the reference in
Baruch to the idols black with the " perpetual smoak
of lamps and incense." In his Hibbert Lectures Professor Rhys refers to churches dedicated to Notre
Dame in virtue of legends of discovery of images of
the Virgin on the spot. These were usually of wood,
which had turned black in the soil. Such a black
" Madonna " was found near Grenoble, in the com-
mune of La Zouche. Then, in the titles of the new
deities, Middleton correctly sees those of the old.
The Queen of Heaven reminds him of Astarte or
Mylitta; the Divine Mother of the Magna Mater,
the " great mother " of Oriental cults. In other attributes of Mary, lineal descendant of Isis, there survive those of Venus, Lucina, Cybele, or Maria. He
gives amusing examples of myths and misreadings
through which certain " saints " have a place in the
Roman Calendar. He apparently knew nothing of the
strange confusion by which Buddha appears therein
under the title of Saint Josaphat; but he tells how, by
misinterpretation of a boundary stone, Proefectus Via-
rum, an overseer of highways, became S. Viar; how
S. Veronica secured canonization through a blunder
over the words Vera Icon: still more droll, how hagi-
ology includes both a mountain and a mantle!

The marks of hands or feet on rocks, said to be made by the apparition of some saint or angel, call to mind " the impression of Hercules' feet on a stone in Scythia "; the picture of the Virgin, which came from heaven, suggests the descent of Numa's shield " from the clouds "; that of the weeping Madonna the statue of Apollo, which Livy says wept for three successive days and nights; while the periodical miracle of the liquefaction of the blood of St. Januarius is obviously paralleled in the incidents named by Horace on his journey to Brundusium, when the priests of the temple at Gnatia sought to persuade him that " the frankincense used to dissolve and melt miraculously without the help of fire " (Sat., v, 97–100).

Middleton, and those of his school, thought that they were near primary formations when they struck on these suggestive classic or pagan parallels to Christian belief and custom. But in truth they had probed a comparatively recent layer; since, far beneath, lay the unsuspected prehistoric deposits of barbaric ideas which are coincident with, and composed of, man's earliest speculations about himself and his surroundings. When, however, we borrow an illustration from geology, it must be remembered that our divisions, like those into which the strata of the globe are separated, are artificial. There is no real detachment. The difference between former and present methods of research is that nowadays we have gone further down for discovery of the common

materials of which barbaric, pagan, and civilized
ideas are compounded. They arise in the comparison
which exists in the savage mind between the living
and the non-living, and in the attribution of like
qualities to things superficially resembling one another; hence belief in their efficacy, which takes
active form in what may be generally termed magic.
For example, the rite of baptism is explained when
we connect it with barbaric lustrations and water-
worship generally; as also that of the Eucharist by
reference to sacrificial feasts in honour of the gods;
feasts at which they were held to be both the eaters
and the eaten. Middleton, himself a clergyman,
shows perplexity when watching the elevation of the
host at mass. He lacked that knowledge of the
origin of sacramental rites which study of barbaric
customs has since supplied. In Mr. Frazer's Golden
Bough, the " central idea " of which is " the conception of the slain god," he shows at what an early
stage in his speculations man formulated the conception of deity incarnated in himself, or in plant or animal, and as afterward slain, both the incarnation and
the death being for the benefit of mankind. The
god is his own sacrifice, and in perhaps the most
striking form, as insisted upon by Mr. Frazer, he is,
as corn-spirit, killed in the person of his representative; the passage in this mode of incarnation to the
custom of eating bread sacramentally being obvious.
The fundamental idea of this sacramental act, as
the mass of examples collected by Mr. Frazer fur-

ther goes to show, is that by eating a thing its physical and mental qualities are acquired. So the barbaric mind reasons, and extends the notion to all beings. To quote Mr. Frazer: " By eating the body of the god he shares in the god's attributes and powers. And when the god is a corn-god, the corn is his proper body; when he is a vine-god, the juice of the grape is his blood; and so by eating the bread and drinking the wine the worshipper partakes of the real body and blood of his god. Thus the drinking of wine in the rites of a vine-god like Dionysus is not an act of revelry; it is a solemn sacrament." It is, perhaps, needless to point out that the same explanation applies to the rites attaching to Demeter, or to add what further parallels are suggested in the belief that Dionysus was slain, rose again, and descended into Hades to bring up his mother Semele from the dead. This, however, by the way. What has to be emphasized is, that in the quotation just given we have transubstantiation clearly anticipated as the barbaric idea of eating the god. In proof of the underlying continuity of that idea two witnesses —Catholic and Protestant—may be cited.

The Church of Rome, and in this the Greek Church is at one therewith, thus defines the term transubstantiation in the Canon of the Council of Trent:

" If any one shall say that in the most holy sacrament of the Eucharist there remains the substance of bread and wine together with the body and blood of our Lord Jesus Christ, and shall deny that wonderful and singular conversion of the whole substance of the bread into the body, and of the whole substance of the wine into the blood, the species of bread and wine alone remaining—which conversion the Catholic Church most fittingly calls Transubstantiation—let him be anathema."

The Church of England, through the medium of a letter to a well-known newspaper, the British Weekly (29th August, 1895), supplies the following illustration of the position of its " High " section, and this, it is interesting to note, from the church of which Mr. Gladstone's son is rector, and in which the distinguished statesman himself often reads the lessons:

" A few Sundays ago—8 o'clock celebration of Holy Communion. Rector, officiating minister (Hawarden Church).

" When the point was reached for the communicants to partake, cards containing a hymn to be sung after Communion were distributed among the congregation. This hymn opened with the following couplet :—

> Jesu, mighty Saviour,
> Thou art *in* us now.

And my attention was arrested by an asterisk referring to a footnote. The word ' in,' in the second line, was printed in italics, and the note intimated that those who had *not* communicated should sing ' *with* ' instead of ' *in*,' i.e. those who had taken the consecrated elements to sing ' Thou art *in* us now,' and those who had not, to sing ' Thou art *with* us now.' "

Whether, therefore, the cult be barbaric or civilized, we find theory and practice identical. The god is eaten so that the communicant thereby becomes a " partaker of the divine nature."

In the gestures denoting *sacerdotal benediction* we

have probably an old form of averting the evil eye; in the act of *breathing* on a bishop at the service of consecration there was the survival of belief in transference of spiritual qualities, the soul being, as language evidences, well-nigh universally identified with breath. The modern spiritualist who describes apparitions as having the " consistency of cigar-smoke," is one with the Congo negroes who leave the house of the dead unswept for a time lest the dust should injure the delicate substance of the ghost. The inhaling of the last breath of the dying Roman by his nearest kinsman has parallel in the breathing of the risen Jesus on his disciples that they might receive the Holy Ghost (John xx, 22). In the offering of *prayers for the dead;* in the *canonization* and *intercession* of *saints;* in the *prayers* and *offerings* at the *shrines of the Virgin* and *saints*, and at the *graves of martyrs;* there are the manifold forms of that great cult of the departed which is found throughout the world. To this may be linked the *belief in angels*, whether good or bad, or guardian, because the element common to the whole is animistic, the peopling of the heavens above, as well as the earth beneath, with an innumerable company of spiritual beings influencing the destinies of men. Well might Jews and Moslems reproach the Christians, as they did down to the eighth century, with having filled the world with more gods than they had overthrown in the pagan temples; while we have Erasmus, in his Encomium Moriae, when reciting the names and functions of saints, add-

ing that " as many things as we wish, so many gods
have we made." Closely related to this group of
beliefs is the *adoration of relics,* the vitality of which
has springs too deep in human nature to be wholly
abolished, whether we carry about us a lock from
the hair of some dead loved one, or read of the fragments of saints or martyrs which lie beneath every
Catholic altar, or of the skull-bones of his ancestor
which the savage carries about with him as a charm.
Then there is the long list of *church festivals,* the
reference of which to pagan prototypes is but one
step toward their ultimate explanation in nature-
worship; there are the *processions* which are the successors of Corybantic frenzies, and, more remotely,
of savage dances and other forms of excitation;
there is that now somewhat casual belief in the
Second Advent which is a member of the widespread
group wherein human hopes fix eyes on the return
of long-sleeping heroes; of Arthur and Olger Dansk,
of Väinämöinen and Quetzalcoatl, of Charlemagne
and Barbarossa, of the lost Marko of Servia and the
lost King Sebastian. We speak of it as " casual,"
because among the two hundred and eighty-odd sects
scheduled in Whitaker's Almanack the curious in
such inquiries will note only three distinctive bodies
of Adventists.

All changes in popular belief have been, and,
practically, remain superficial; the old animism pervades the higher creeds. In our own island, for example, the Celtic and pre-Celtic paganism remained

unleavened by the old Roman religion. The legions took back to Rome the gods which they brought with them. The names of Mithra and Serapis occur on numerous tablets, the worship of the one—that " Sol invictus " whose birthday at the winter solstice became (see p. 42) the anniversary of the birth of Christ—had ranged as far west as South Wales and Northumberland; while the foundations of a temple to the other have been unearthed at York. The chief Celtic gods, in virtue of common attributes as elemental nature-deities, were identified with certain *dii majores* of the Roman pantheon, and the *deae matres* equated with the gracious or malevolent spirits of the indigenous faith. But the old names were not displaced. Neither did the earlier Christian missionaries effect any organic change in popular beliefs, while, during the submergence of Christianity under waves of barbaric invasion, there were infused into the old religion kindred elements from oversea which gave it yet more vigorous life. The eagle penetration of Gibbon detected this persistent element at work when he described the sequel to the futile efforts of Theodosius to extirpate paganism. The ancestor worship which lay at the core of much of it took shape among the Christianized pagans in the worship of martyrs and in the scramble after their relics. The bodies of prophets and apostles were discovered by the strangest coincidences, and transported to the churches by the Tiber and the Bosphorus, and although the supply of these more important remains was soon exhausted, there was no limit to the production of relics of their person or belongings, as of filings from the chains of S. Peter, and from the gridiron of S. Lawrence. The catacombs yielded any number of the bodies of martyrs, and Rome became a huge manufactory to meet the demands for wonder-working relics from every part of Christendom. A sceptical feeling might be aroused at the claims of a dozen abbeys to possession of the veritable crown of thorns wherewith the majesty of the suffering Christ was mocked, but it was silenced before the numerous fragments of his cross, since ingenuity has computed that this must have contained at least one hundred and eighty million cubic millemetres, whereas the total cubic volume of all the known relics is but five millions. "It must," remarks Gibbon (Decline and Fall, end of chap. xxviii), " ingeniously be confessed that the ministers of the Catholic Church imitated the profane model which they were impotent to destroy. The most respectable bishops had persuaded themselves that the ignorant rustics would more cheerfully renounce the superstitions of paganism if they found some resemblance, some compensation, in the bosom of Christianity. The religion of Constantine achieved, in less than a century, the final conquest of the Roman Empire, but the victors themselves were insensibly subdued by the arts of their vanquished rivals."

Enough has been said on a topic to which prominence has been given because it brings into fuller relief the fact that in a religion for which its apologists claim divine origin and guidance " to the end of the world " we have the same intrusion of the rites and customs of lower cults which marks other advanced faiths. Hence, science and superstition being deadly foes, the explanation of that hostile attitude toward inquiry and that dread of its results which marked Christianity down to modern times. While the intrusion of corrupting elements presents difficulties which the theory of the supernatural history of Christianity alone creates, it accords with all that might be predicted of a religion whose success was due to its early escape from the narrow confines of Judaism; and to its fortunate contact with the enterprising peoples to whom the civilization of Europe and the New World is due.

2. *From Augustine to Lord Bacon.*
A. D. 400–A. D. 1600.

The foregoing slight outline of the causes which operated for centuries against the freedom of the human mind will render it needless to follow the history of the development of Christian polity and dogma—the temporalizing of the one, and the crystallizing of the other. Yet one prominent actor in that history demands a brief notice, because of the influence which his teaching wielded from the fifth to the fifteenth centuries. The annals of the churches in Africa, along whose northern shores Christianity had spread early and rapidly, yield notable names,

6

but none so distinguished as that of Augustine, Bishop of Hippo from 395 to 430 A. D. This greatest of the Fathers of the Church sought, as has been remarked already, to bring the system of Aristotle, the greatest of ancient naturalists, into line with Christian theology. His range of study was well-nigh as wide as that of the famous Stagirite, but we are here concerned only with so much of it as bears on an attempt to graft the development theory on the dogma of special creation. Augustine, accepting the Old Testament cosmogony as a revelation, believed that the world was created out of nothing, but, this initial paradox accepted, he argued that God had endowed matter with certain powers of self-development which left free the operation of natural causes in the production of plants and animals. With this, however, as already noted, he held, with preceding philosophers and with his fellow-theologians, the doctrine of spontaneous generation. It explained to him the existence of apparently purposeless creatures, as flies, frogs, mice, etc. "Certain very small animals," he says, "may not have been created on the fifth and sixth days, but may have originated later from putrefying matter." Not till the seventeenth century did the experiments of Redi refute a doctrine which had held part of the biological field for above two thousand years, and which still has adherents. Of course Augustine, as do modern Catholic biologists, excepted man from the operation of secondary causes, and held that his

soul was created by the direct intervention of the
Creator. Augustine's concessions are, therefore,
more seeming than real, and, moreover, we find him
denying the existence of the antipodes on the ground
that Scripture is silent about them, and also, that if
God had placed any races there, they could not see
Christ descending at his second coming. To Augustine the air was full of devils who are the cause of
" all diseases of Christians." In other words, he was
not ahead of the illusions of his age.] Then, too,
he shows that allegorizing spirit which was manifest
in Greece a thousand years earlier; the spirit which
reads hidden meanings in Homer, in Horace, and in
Omar Khayyám; and which, in the hands of present-
day Gnostics, mostly fantastic or illiterate cabalists,
converts the plain narratives of Old and New Testa-
ments into vehicles of mysterious types and esoteric
symbols. It is in such allegorical vein that Augustine explains the outside and inside pitching of the
ark as typifying the safety of the Church from the
leaking-in of heresy; while the ghastly application
of symbolical exegetics is seen in his citation of the
words of Jesus, " Compel them to come in," as a Divine warrant for the slaughter of heretics.

We shall meet with no other such commanding
figure in Church history till nine hundred years have
passed, when Thomas Aquinas, the " Angel of the
Schools," appears, but although that period marks
no advance of the Church from her central position,
it witnessed changes in her fortune through the in-

trusion of a strange people into her territory and
sanctuaries.

Perhaps there are few events in history more
impressive than the conversion of the wild and ignorant Arab tribes of the seventh century from stone-
worship to monotheism.   The series of conquests
which followed had also, as an indirect and unfore-
seen result, effects of vast importance in the revival
and spread of Greek culture from the Tigris to the
Guadalquivir.   It is not easy, neither does the inquiry fall within our present purpose, to discover the
special impulses which led Mohammed, the leader
of the movement, to preach a new faith whose one
creed, stripped of all subtleties, was the unity of God.
Large numbers of Jews and Christians had settled
in Arabia long before his time, and he had become
acquainted with the narrowness of the one, and with
the causes of the wranglings of the other, riven, as
these last-named were, into sects quarrelling over
the nature of the Person of Christ.   These, and the
fetichism of his fellow-countrymen, may, perhaps,
have impelled him to start a crusade the mandate
for which he, in fanatic impulse, believed came from
heaven.   The result is well known.   The hitherto
untamed nomads became the eager instruments of
the prophet.   Under his leadership, and that of the
able Khalifs who succeeded him, the flag of Islam
was carried from East to West, till within one hundred years of the flight of Mohammed from Mecca

(622 A. D.) it waved from the Indian Ocean to the Atlantic. With the conquest of Syria there was achieved one of the greatest and most momentous of triumphs in the capture of Jerusalem, and the seizure of sites sanctified to Christians by association with the crucifixion, burial, and resurrection of Jesus. Only a few years before (614 A. D.), the holy city had been taken by Chosroes; the sacred buildings raised over the venerated tomb had been burned, and the cross—a spurious relic—carried off by the Persian king. These places have been, as it were, the cockpit of Christendom from the time of the siege of Jerusalem under Titus to that of the Crimean war, when blood was spilt like water in a conflict stirred by squabbles between Latin and Greek Christians over possession of the key of the Church of the Nativity at Bethlehem. In the Church of the Holy Sepulchre these sectaries are still kept from flying at one another's throats by the muskets of Mohammedan soldiers.

The Arabian conquest of Persia followed that of Syria. The turn of Egypt soon came, the city of Alexandria being taken in 640, seven years after the prophets' death. Since the loss of Greek freedom, and the decay of intellectual life at Athens, that renowned place had become, notably under the Ptolemies, the chief home of science and philosophy. Through the propagandism of Christianity among the Hellenized Jews, of whom, as of Greeks, large numbers had settled there, it was also the birthplace of dogmatic theology, and, therefore, the fountain whence welled the controversies whose logomachies were the gossip of the streets of Constantinople and the cause of bloody persecution. After a few years' pause, the Saracens (Ar., *sharkiin,* orientals) resumed their conquering march. They captured and burnt Carthage, another famous centre of Christianity, and then crossed over to Spain. In "the fair and fertile isle of Andalusia" the Gothic king Roderick was aroused from his luxurious life in Toledo to lead his army in gallant, but vain, attempt to repel the infidel invaders. So rapid was their advance that in six years they had subdued the whole of Spain, the north and northwestern portions excepted, for the hardy Basque mountaineers maintained their independence against the Arabs, as they had maintained it against Celt, Roman, and Goth. Only before the walls of Tours did the invaders meet with a rebuff from Charles Martel and his Franks, which arrested their advance in Western Europe; as, in a more momentous defeat before Constantinople by Leo III. in 718, fourteen years earlier, the torrent of Mohammedan conquest was first checked.

Enough, however, of Saracenic wars and their destructive work, which, if tradition lies not, included the burning of the remnants of the vast Alexandrian library. "A revealed dogma is always opposed to the free research that may contradict it," and Islam has ever been a worse foe to science than Christianity. Its association, as a religion, with the renaissance of knowledge, was as wholly accidental as the story of it is interesting.

Under the Sassanian kings, Persia had become an active centre of intellectual life, reaching the climax of its Augustan age in the reign of Chosroes. Jew, Greek, and Christian alike had welcome at his court, and translations of the writings of the Indian sages completed the eclecticism of that enlightened monarch. Then came the ruthless Arab, and philosophy and science were eclipsed. But with the advent of the Abbaside Khalifs, who number the famous Haroun al-Raschid among them, there came revival of the widest toleration, and consequent return of intellectual activity. Baghdad arose as the seat of empire. Situated on the high road of Oriental commerce, along which travelled foreign ideas and foreign culture, that city became also the Oxford of her time. Arabic was the language of the conquerors, and into that poetic, but unphilosophic, tongue, Greek philosophy and science were rendered. Under the rule of those Khalifs, says Renan, " nontolerant, nonreluctant persecutors," free thought developed; the *Motecallenim* or " disputants " held debates, where all religions were examined in the light of reason. Aristotle, Euclid, Galen, and Ptolemy were textbooks in the colleges, the repute of whose teachers brought to Baghdad and Naishapur (dear to lovers of " old " Khayyám) students westward from Spain, and eastward from Transoxiana.

" Arab " philosophy, therefore, is only a name.

It has been well described as "a system of Greek thought expressed in a Semitic tongue; and modified by Oriental influences called into existence by the patronage of the more liberal princes, and kept alive by the zeal of a small band of thinkers." In the main, it began and ended with the study of Aristotle, commentaries on whom became the chief work of scholars, at whose head stands the great name of Averroes. Through these—a handful of Jews and Moslems—knowledge of Greek science, of astronomy, algebra, chemistry, and medicine, was carried into Western Europe. By the latter half of the tenth century, one hundred and fifty years after the translation of Aristotle into Arabic, Spain had become no mean rival of Baghdad and Cairo. Schools were founded; colleges to which the Girton girls of the period could repair to learn mathematics and history were set up by lady principals; manufactures and agriculture were encouraged; and lovely and stately palaces and mosques beautified Seville, Cordova, Toledo, and Granada, which last-named city the far-famed Alhâmra or Red Fortress still overlooks. Seven hundred years before there was a public lamp in London, and when Paris was a town of swampy roadways bordered by windowless dwellings, Cordova had miles of well-lighted, well-paved streets; and the constant use of the bath by the "infidel" contrasted with the saintly filth and rags which were the pride of flesh-mortifying devotees and the outward and odorous signs of their religion. The pages

of our dictionaries evidence in familiar mathematical
and chemical terms; in the names of the principal
" fixed " stars; and in the words " admiral " and
" chemise "; the influence of the " Arab " in science,
war, and dress.

It forms no part of our story to tell how feuds
between rival dynasties and rival sects of Islam,
becoming more acute as time went on, enabled Christianity to recover lost ground, and, in the capture
of Granada in 1492, to put an end to Moorish rule
in Spain. Before that event, a knowledge of Greek
philosophy had been diffused through Christendom
by the translation of the works of Avicenna, Averroes, and other scholars, into Latin. That was about
the middle of the twelfth century, when Aristotle,
who had been translated into Arabic some three centuries earlier, also appeared in Latin dress. The
detachment of any branch of knowledge from theology being a thing undreamed of, the deep reverence in which the Stagirite was held by his Arabian
commentators ultimately led to his becoming " sus-
pect " by the Christians, since that which approved
itself to the followers of Mohammed must, *ipso facto*,
be condemned by the followers of Jesus. Hence
came reaction, and recourse to the Scriptures as sole
guide to secular as well as sacred knowledge; recourse to a method which, as Hallam says, " had not
untied a single knot, or added one unequivocal truth
to the domain of philosophy."

So far as the scanty records tell (for we may

never know how much was suppressed, or fell into oblivion, under ecclesiastical frowns and threats; nor how many thinkers toiled in secret and in dread), none seemed possessed either of courage or desire to supplement the revealed word by examination into things themselves. To supplant it was not dreamed of. But, in the middle of the thirteenth century, one notable exception occurred in the person of Roger Bacon, sometimes called Friar Bacon in virtue of his belonging to the order of Franciscans. He was born in 1214 at Ilchester, in Somerset, whence he afterward removed to Oxford, and thence to Paris. That this remarkable and many-sided man, classic and Arabic scholar, mathematician, and natural philosopher, has not a more recognised place in the annals of science is strange, although it is, perhaps, partly explained by the fact that his writings were not reissued for more than three centuries after his death. He has been credited with a number of inventions, his title to which is however doubtful, although the doubt in nowise impairs the greatness of his name. He shared the current belief in alchemy, but made a number of experiments in chemistry pointing to his knowledge of the properties of the various gases, and of the components of gunpowder. If he did not invent spectacles, or the microscope and telescope, he was skilled in optics, and knew the principles on which those instruments are made, as the following extract from his Opus Majus shows: "We can place transparent bodies in such a form and position between our eyes and other objects that the rays shall be refracted and bent toward any place we please, so that we shall see the object near at hand, or at a distance, under any angle we please; and thus from an incredible distance we may read the smallest letters, and may number the smallest particles of sand, by reason of the greatness of the angle under which they appear." He knew the " wisdom of the ancients " in the cataloguing of the stars, and suggested a reform of the calendar—following the then unknown poet-astronomer of Naishapur. But he believed in astrology, that bastard science which from remotest times had ruled the life of man, and which has no small number of votaries among ourselves to this day. Roger Bacon's abiding title to fame rests, however, on his insistence on the necessity of experiment, and his enforcement of this precept by practice. As a mathematician he laid stress on the application of this " first of all the sciences "; indeed, as " preceding all others, and as disposing us to them." His experiments, both from their nature and the seclusion in which they were made, laid him open to the charge of black magic, in other words, of being in league with the devil. This, in the hands of a theology thus " possessed," became an instrument of awful torture to mankind. Roger Bacon's denial of magic only aggravated his crime, since in ecclesiastical ears, this was tantamount to a denial of the activity, nay more, of the very .existence of Satan. So, despite certain encouragement in his scientific work from an old friend who afterward became Pope Clement IV., for whose information he wrote his Opus Majus, he was, on the death of that potentate, thrown into prison, whence tradition says he emerged, after ten years, only to die.

The theories of mediæval schoolmen—a monotonous record of unprogressive ideas—need not be scheduled here, the more so as we approach the period of discoveries momentous in their ultimate effect upon opinions which now possess only the value attaching to the history of discredited conceptions of the universe. Commerce, more than scientific curiosity, gave the impetus to the discovery that the earth is a globe. Trade with the East was divided between Genoa and Venice. These cities were rivals, and the Genoese, alarmed at the growing success of the Venetians, resolved to try to reach India from the west. Their schemes were justified by reports of land indications brought by seamen who had passed through the " Pillars of Hercules " to the Atlantic. The sequel is well known. Columbus, after clerical opposition, and rebuffs from other states, " offering," as Mr. Payne says, in his excellent History of America, " though he knew it not, the New World in exchange for three ships and provisions for twelve months," finally secured the support of the Spanish king, and sailed from Cadiz on the 3d of August, 1492. On 11th of October he sighted the fringes of the New World, and believing

that he had sailed from Spain to India, gave the name
West Indies to the island-group. America itself had
been discovered by roving Norsemen five hundred
years before, but the fact was buried in Icelandic
tradition. Following Columbus, Vasco de Gama, a
Portuguese, set sail in 1497, and taking a southerly
course, doubled the Cape of Good Hope. Twenty-
two years later, Ferdinand Magellan started on a
voyage more famous than that of Columbus, since
his ambition was to sail round the world, and thus
complete the chain of proof against the theory of its
flatness. For "though the Church hath evermore
from Holy Writ affirmed that the earth should be a
widespread plain bordered by the waters, yet he
comforted himself when he considered that in the
eclipses of the moon the shadow cast of the earth is
round; and as is the shadow, such, in like manner,
is the substance." Doubling Cape Horn through
the straits that bear his name, Magellan entered the
vast ocean whose calm surface caused him to call it
the Pacific, and after terrible sufferings, he reached
the Ladrone Islands where, either at the hands of a
mutinous crew, or of savages, he was killed. His
chief lieutenant, Sebastian d'Eleano, continued the
voyage, and after rounding the Cape of Good Hope,
brought the San Vittoria—name of happy omen—
to anchor at St. Lucar, near Seville, on 7th of Sep-
tember, 1522. Brought, too, the story of a circum-
navigated globe, and of new groups of stars never
seen under northern skies.

The scene shifts, for the time being, from the earth to the heavens. The Church had barely recovered from the blow struck at her authority on matters of secular knowledge, when another dealt, and that by an ecclesiastic, Copernicus, Canon of Frauenburg, in Prussia. But before pursuing this, some reference to the revolt against the Church of Rome, which is the great event of the sixteenth century, is necessary, if only to inquire whether the movement known as the Reformation justified its name as freeing the intellect from theological thraldom. Far-reaching as were the areas which it covered and the effects which it wrought, its quarrel with the Church of Rome was not because of that Church's attitude toward freedom of thought. On the Continent it was a protest of nobler minds against the corruptions fostered by the Papacy; in England, it was personal and political in origin, securing popular support by its anti-sacerdotal character, and its appeal to national irritation against foreign control. But, both here and abroad, it sought mending rather than ending; " not to vary in any jot from the faith Catholic." It disputed the claim of the Church to be the sole interpreter of Scripture, and contended that such interpretation was the right and duty of the individual. But it would not admit the right of the individual to call in question the authority of the Bible itself: to that book alone must a man go for knowledge of things temporal as of things spiritual. So that the Reformation was but an exchange of

fetters, or, as Huxley happily puts it, the scraping
of a little rust off the chains which still bound the
mind. "Learning perished where Luther reigned,"
said Erasmus, and in proof of it we find the Reformer agreeing with his coadjutor, Melanchthon, in
permitting no tampering with the written Word.
Copernicus notwithstanding, they had no doubt that
the earth was fixed and that sun and stars travelled
round it, because the Bible said so. Peter Martyr,
one of the early Lutheran converts, in his Com-
mentary on Genesis, declared that wrong opinions
about the creation as narrated in that book would
render valueless all the promises of Christ. Wherein
he spoke truly. As for the schoolmen, Luther called
them "locusts, caterpillars, frogs, and lice." Reason he denounced as the "arch whore" and the
"devil's bride," Aristotle is a "prince of darkness,
horrid impostor, public and professed liar, beast, and
twice execrable." Consistently enough, Luther believed vehemently in a personal devil, and in witches;
"I would myself burn them," he says, "even as it is
written in the Bible that the priests stoned offenders."
To him demoniacal possession was a fact clear as
noonday: idiocy, lunacy, epilepsy and all other mental and nervous disorders were due to it. Hence,
a movement whose intent appeared to be the freeing of the human spirit riveted more tightly the
bolts that imprisoned it; arresting the physical explanation of mental diseases and that curative treatment of them which is one of the countless services

of science to suffering mankind. To Luther, the
descent of Christ into hell, which modern research
has shown to be a variant of an Orphic legend of
the underworld, was a real event, Jesus going thither
that he might conquer Satan in a hand-to-hand
struggle.

Therefore, freedom of thought, as we define it,
had the bitterest foe in Luther, although, in his con-
demnation of " works," and his fanatical dogma of
man's " justification by faith alone," which made
him reject the Epistle of James as one " of straw,"
and as unworthy of a. place in the Canon, he unwittingly drove in the thin end of the rationalist wedge.
The Reformers had hedged the canonical books with
theories of verbal inspiration which extended even
to the punctuation of the sentences. They thus rendered intelligent study of the Bible impossible, and
did grievous injury to a collection of writings of vast
historical value, and of abiding interest as records
of man's primitive speculations and spiritual development. But Luther's application of the right of
private judgment to the omission or addition of this
or that book into a canon which had been closed by
a Council of the Church, surrendered the whole position, since there was no telling where the thing might
stop.

Copernicus waited full thirty years before he ven-
tured to make his theory public. The Ptolemaic
system, which assumed a fixed earth with sun, moon,
and stars revolving above it, had held the field for

about fourteen hundred years. It accorded with Scripture; it was adopted by the Church; and, moreover, it was confirmed by the senses, the correction of which still remains, and will long remain, a condition of intellectual advance. Little wonder is it, then, that Copernicus hesitated to broach a theory thus supported, or that, when published, it was put forth in tentative form as a possible explanation more in accord with the phenomena. A preface, presumably by a friendly hand, commended the Revolutions of the Heavenly Bodies to Pope Paul III. It urged that " as in previous times others had been allowed the privilege of feigning what circles they chose in order to explain the phenomena," Copernicus " had conceived that he might take the liberty of trying whether, on the supposition of the earth's motion, it was possible to find better explanations than the ancient ones of the revolutions of the celestial orbs." A copy of the book was placed in the hands of its author only a few hours before his death on 23d of May, 1543.

This " upstart astrologer," this " fool who wishes to reverse the entire science of astronomy," for " sacred Scripture tells us that Joshua commanded the sun to stand still, and not the earth "—these are Luther's words—was, therefore, beyond the grip of the Holy Inquisition. But a substitute was forthcoming. Giordano Bruno, a Dominican monk, had added to certain heterodox beliefs the heresy of Copernicanism, which he publicly taught from Oxford

7

to Venice. For these cumulative crimes he was imprisoned and, after two years, condemned to be put to death " as mercifully as possible and without the shedding of his blood," a Catholic euphemism for burning a man alive. The murder was committed in Rome on 17th of February, 1600.

The year 1543 marks an epoch in biology as in astronomy. As shown in the researches of Galen, an Alexandrian physician of the second century, there had been no difficulty in studying the structure of the lower animals, but, fortified both by tradition and by prejudice, the Church refused to permit dissection of the human body, and in the latter part of the thirteenth century, Boniface VIII. issued a Bull of the major excommunication against offenders. Prohibition, as usual, led to evasion, and Vesalius, Professor of Anatomy in Padua University, resorted to various devices to procure " subjects," the bodies of criminals being easiest to obtain. The end justified the means, as he was able to correct certain errors of Galen, and to give the *quietus* to the old legend, based upon the myth of the creation of Eve, that man has one rib less than woman. This was among the discoveries announced in his De Corporis Humani Fabrica, published when he was only twenty-eight years of age. The book fell under the ban of the Church because Vesalius gave no support to the belief in an indestructible bone, nucleus of the resurrection body, in man. The belief had, no doubt, near relation to that of the Jews in the *os sacru,* and may remind us of Descartes' fanciful location of the soul in the minute cone-like part of the brain known as the *conarium,* or pineal gland. On some baseless charge of attempting the dissection of a living subject, the Inquisition haled Vesalius to prison, and would have put him to death " as mercifully as possible," but for the intervention of King Charles V. of Spain, to whom Vesalius had been physician. Returning in October, 1564, from a pilgrimage taken, presumably, as atonement for his alleged offence, he was shipwrecked on the coast of Zante, and died of exhaustion.

While the heretical character and tendencies of discoveries in astronomy and anatomy awoke active opposition from the Church, the work of men of the type of Gesner, the eminent Swiss naturalist, and of Caesalpino, professor of botany at Padua, passed unquestioned. No dogma was endangered by the classification of plants and animals. But when a couple of generations after the death of Copernicus had passed, the Inquisition found a second victim in the famous Galileo, who was born at Pisa in 1564. After spending some years in mechanical and mathematical pursuits, he began a series of observations in confirmation of the Copernican theory, of the truth of which he had been convinced in early life. With the aid of a rude telescope, made by his own hands, he discovered the satellites of Jupiter; the moon-like phases of Venus and Mars; mountains and valleys in the moon; spots on the sun's disk; and the countless stars which composed the luminous band known as the Milky Way. Nought occurred to disturb his observations till, in a work on the Solar Spots, he explained the movements of the earth and of the heavenly bodies according to Copernicus. On the appearance of that book the authorities contented themselves with a caution to the author. But action followed his supplemental Dialogue on the Copernican and Ptolemaic Systems. Through that convenient medium which the title implies, Galileo makes the defender of the Copernican theory an easy victor, and for this he was brought before the Inquisition in 1633. After a tedious trial, and threats of " rigorous personal examination," a euphemism for " torture," he was, despite the plea—too specious to deceive—that he had merely put the *pros* and *cons* as between the rival theories, condemned to abjure all that he had taught. There is a story, probably fictitious, since it was first told in 1789, that when the old man rose from his knees, he muttered his conviction that the earth moves, in the words " e pur si muove." As a sample of the arguments used by the ecclesiastics when they substituted, as rare exception, the pen for the faggot, the reasoning advanced by one Sizzi against the existence of Jupiter's moons, may be cited. " There are seven windows given to animals in the domicile of the head, through which the air is admitted to the tabernacle of the body, viz.: two nostrils, two eyes, two ears, and one mouth. So, in the heavens, as in a macrocosm, or great world, there are two favourable stars, Jupiter and Venus; two unpropitious, Mars and Saturn; two luminaries, the sun and moon, and Mercury alone undecided and indifferent. From these and many other phenomena of Nature, which it were tedious to enumerate, we gather that the number of planets is necessarily seven. Moreover, the satellites are invisible to the naked eye, and, therefore, can exercise no influence over the earth, and would, of course, be useless; and, therefore, do not exist."

In this brief summary of the attitude of the Church toward science, it is not possible, and if it were so, it is not needful, to refer in detail to the contributions of the more speculative philosophers, who, although they made no discoveries, advocated those methods of research and directions of inquiry which made the discoveries possible. Among these a prominent name is that of Lord Bacon, whose system of philosophy, known as the Inductive, proceeds from the collection, examination and comparison of any group of connected facts to the relation of them to some general principle. The universal is thus explained by the particular. But the inductive method was no invention of Bacon's; wherever observation or testing of a thing preceded speculation about it, as with his greater namesake, there the Baconian system had its application. Lord Bacon, moreover, undervalued Greek science; he argued against the Copernican theory; and either knew nothing of, or ignored, Harvey's momentous discov-

ery of the circulation of the blood. A more illustrious
name than his is that of René Descartes, a man who
combined theory with observation; " one who," in
Huxley's words, " saw that the discoveries of Galileo
meant that the remotest parts of the universe were
governed by mechanical laws, while those of Harvey
meant that the same laws presided over the operations of that portion of the world which is nearest to
us, namely, our own bodily frame." The greatness
of this man, a good Catholic, whom the Jesuits
charged with Atheism, has no mean tribute in his
influence on an equally remarkable man, Benedict
Spinoza. Spinoza reduced the Cartesian analysis of
phenomena into God, mind and matter to one phenomenon, namely, God, of whom matter and spirit,
extension and thought, are but attributes. His short
life fell within the longer span of Newton's, whose
strange subjection to the theological influences of
his age is seen in this immortal interpreter of the
laws of the universe wasting his later years on an
attempt to interpret unfulfilled prophecy. These and
others, as Locke, Leibnitz, Herder, and Schelling,
like the great Hebrew leader, had glimpses of a
goodly land which they were not themselves to
enter. But, perhaps, in the roll of illustrious men
to whom prevision came, none have better claim to
everlasting remembrance than Immanuel Kant. For
in his Theory of the Heavens, published in 1755, he
anticipates that hypothesis of the origin of the present universe which, associated with the succeeding

names of Laplace and Herschel, has, under correc-
tions furnished by modern physics, common acceptance among us. Then, as shown in the following
extract, Kant foresees the theory of the development
of life from formless stuff to the highest types: " It
is desirable to examine the great domain of organized
beings by means of a methodical comparative anatomy, in order to discover whether we may not find
in them something resembling a system, and that
too in connection with their mode of generation, so
that we may not be compelled to stop short with a
mere consideration of forms as they are—which gives
no insight into their generation—and need not despair of gaining a full insight into this department of
Nature. The agreement of so many kinds of animals
in a certain common plan of structure, which seems
to be visible not only in their skeletons, but also in
the arrangement of the other parts—so that a won-
derfully simple typical form, by the shortening or
lengthening of some parts, and by the suppression
and development of others, might be able to produce
an immense variety of species—gives us a ray of
hope, though feeble, that here perhaps some results
may be obtained, by the application of the principle
of the mechanism of Nature; without which, in fact,
no science can exist. This analogy of forms (in so
far as they seem to have been produced in accordance
with a common prototype, notwithstanding their
great variety) strengthens the supposition that they
have an actual blood-relationship, due to derivation

from a common parent; a supposition which is arrived at by observation of the graduated approximation of one class of animals to another, beginning
with the one in which the principle of purposiveness
seems to be most conspicuous, namely, man, and extending down to the polyps, and from these even
down to mosses and lichens, and arriving finally at
raw matter, the lowest stage of Nature observable
by us.   From this raw matter and its forces, the
whole apparatus of Nature seems to have been derived according to mechanical laws (such as those
which resulted in the production of crystals); yet this
apparatus, as seen in organic beings, is so incomprehensible to us, that we feel ourselves compelled to
conceive for it a different principle.   But it would
seem that the archæologist of Nature is at liberty to
regard the great Family of creatures (for as a Family
we must conceive it, if the above-mentioned continuous and connected relationship has a real foundation)
as having sprung from their immediate results of her
earliest revolutions, judging from all the laws of
their mechanisms known to or conjectured by him."

In our arrival at the age of these seers, we feel
the play of a freer, purer air; a lull in the miasmatic
currents that bring intolerance on their wings.   The
tolerance that approaches is due to no surrender of
its main position by dogmatic theology, but to that
larger perception of the variety and complexity of
life, ignorance of, or wilful blindness to, which is the
secret of the survival of rigid opinion.   The demon-

stration of the earth's roundness; the discovery of
America; the growing conception of inter-relation
between the lowest and the highest life-forms; the
slow but sure acceptance of the Copernican theory;
and, above all, the idea of a Cosmos, an unbroken
order, to which every advance in knowledge con-
tributes, justified and fostered the free play of the
intellect. Foreign as yet, however, to the minds of
widest breadth, was the conception of the inclusion
of MAN himself in the universal order. Duality—
Nature overruled by supernature—was the unaltered
note; the supernature as part of Nature a thing undreamed of. Nor could it be otherwise while the
belief in diabolical agencies still held the field, send-
ing wretched victims to the stake on the evidence
of conscientious witnesses, and with the concurrence
of humane judges. Animism, the root of all per-
sonification, whether of good or evil, had lost none
of its essential character, and but little of its vigour.

" I flatter myself," says Hume, in the opening
words of the essay upon Miracles, in his Inquiry
Concerning Human Understanding, " that I have
discovered an argument of a like nature (he is referring to Archbishop Tillotson's argument on Transubstantiation) which, if just, will, with the wise and
learned, be an everlasting check to all kind of superstitious delusion, and, consequently, will be useful
as long as the world endures." Hume certainly did
not overrate the force of the blow which he dealt at
supernaturalism, one of a series of attacks which, in

France and Britain, carried the war into the camp of the enemy, and changed its tactics from aggressive to defensive. But none the less is it true that the " superstitious delusions " against which he planted his logical artillery were killed neither by argument nor by evidence. Delusion and error do not perish by controversial warfare. They perish under the slow and silent operation of changes to which they are unable to adapt themselves. The atmosphere is altered: the organism can neither respond nor respire; therefore, it dies. Thus, save where lurks the ignorance which is its breath of life, has wholly perished belief in witchcraft; thus, too, is slowly perishing belief in miracles, and, with this, belief in the miraculous events, the incarnation, resurrection, and ascension of Jesus, on which the fundamental tenets of Christianity are based, and in which lies so largely the secret of its long hostility to knowledge.

PART III.

THE RENASCENCE OF SCIENCE.

A. D. 1600 ONWARDS.

"Though science, like Nature, may be driven out with a fork,
ecclesiastical or other, yet she surely comes back again."—
HUXLEY, Prologue to Collected Essays, vol. v.

THE exercise of a more tolerant spirit, to which
reference has been made, had its limits. It is true
that Dr. South, a famous divine, denounced the
Royal Society (founded 1645) as an irreligious body;
although a Dr. Wallis, one of the first members, especially declared that "matters of theology" were
"precluded": the business being "to discourse and
consider of philosophical inquiries and such as related thereunto; as Physick, Anatomy, Geometry,
Astronomy, Navigation, Staticks, Magneticks, Chym-
icks, and Natural Experiments; with the state of these
studies, and their cultivation at home and abroad."
Regardless of South and such as agreed with him,
Torricelli worked at hydrodynamics, and discovered
the principle of the barometer; Boyle inquired into
the law of the compressibility of gases; Malpighi
examined minute life-forms and the structure of organs under the microscope; Ray and Willughby
classified plants and animals; Newton theorized on

the nature of light; and Roemer measured its speed; Halley estimated the sun's distance, predicted the return of comets, and observed the transits of Venus and Mercury; Hunter dissected specimens, and laid the foundations of the science of comparative anatomy; and many another illustrious worker contributed to the world's stock of knowledge " without let or hindrance," for in all this " matters of theology were precluded."

But the old spirit of resistance was aroused when, after a long lapse of time, inquiry was revived in a branch of science which, it will be noticed, has no distinct place in the subjects dealt with by the Royal Society at the start. That science was Geology; a science destined, in its ultimate scope, to prove a far more powerful dissolvent of dogma than any of its compeers.

It seems strange that the discovery of the earth's true shape and movements was not sooner followed by investigation into her contents, but the old ideas of special creation remained unaffected by these and other discoveries, and the more or less detailed account of the process of creation furnished in the book of Genesis sufficed to arrest curiosity. In the various departments of the inorganic universe the earth was the last to become subject of scientific research; as in study of the organic universe, man excluded himself till science compelled his inclusion.

After more than two thousand years, the Ionian philosophers " come to their own " again. Xenophanes of Colophon has been referred to as arriving, five centuries B. C., at a true explanation of the imprints of plants and animals in rocks. Pythagoras, who lived before him, may, if Ovid, writing near the Christian era, is to be trusted, have reached some sound conclusions about the action of water in the changes of land and sea areas. But we are on surer ground when we meet the geographer Strabo, who lived in the reign of Augustus. Describing the countries in which he travelled, he notes their various features, and explains the causes of earthquakes and allied phenomena. Then eleven hundred years pass before we find any explanation of like rational character supplied. This was furnished by the Arabian philosopher, Avicenna, whose theory of the origin of mountains is the more marvellous when we remember what intellectual darkness surrounded him. He says that " mountains may be due to two different causes. Either they are effects of upheavals of the crust of the earth, such as might occur during a violent earthquake, or they are the effect of water, which, cutting for itself a new route, has denuded the valleys, the strata being of different kinds, some soft, some hard. The winds and waters disintegrate the one, but leave the other intact. Most of the eminences of the earth have had this latter origin. It would require a long period of time for all such changes to be accomplished, during which the mountains themselves might be somewhat diminished in size. But that water has been the main cause of

these effects is proved by the existence of fossil remains of aquatic and other animals on many mountains " (cf. Osborn's From the Greeks to Darwin,
p. 76). A similar explanation of fossils was given
by the engineer-artist Leonardo de Vinci in the fifteenth century, and by the potter Bernard Palissy,
in the sixteenth century; but thence onward, for
more than a hundred years, the earth was as a sealed
book to man. The earlier chapters of its history,
once reopened, have never been closed again. Varied
as were the theories of the causes which wrought
manifold changes on its surface, they agreed in de-
manding a far longer time-history than the Church
was willing to allow. If the reasoning of the geologists was sound, the narrative in Genesis was a myth.
Hence the renewal of struggle between the Christian
Church and Science, waged, at first, over the six
days of the Creation.

Here and there, in bygone days, a sceptical voice
had been raised in denial of the Mosaic authorship
of the Pentateuch. Such was that of La Peyrère
who, in 1655, published an instalment of a work in
which he anticipated what is nowadays accepted,
but what then was akin to blasphemy to utter. For
not only does he doubt whether Moses had any
hand in the writings attributed to him: he rejects
the orthodox view of suffering and death as the
penalties of Adam's disobedience; and gives rational-
istic interpretation of the appearance of the star of
Bethlehem, and of the darkness at the Crucifixion.

But La Peyrère became a Roman Catholic, and, of course, recanted his opinions. Then, nearer the time when controversy on the historical character of the Scriptures was becoming active, one Astruc,a French physician, suggested, in a work published in 1753, that Moses may have used older materials in his compilation of the earlier parts of the Pentateuch.

But, practically, the five books included under that name, were believed to have been written by Moses under divine authority. The statement in Genesis that God made the universe and its contents, both living and non-living, in six days of twenty-four hours each, was explicit. Thus interpreted, as their plain meaning warranted, Archbishop Usher made his famous calculation as to the time elapsing between the creation and the birth of Christ. Dr. White, in his important Warfare of Science with Theology, gives an amusing example of the application of Usher's method in detail. A seventeenth century divine, Dr. Lightfoot, Vice-Chancellor of Cambridge University, computed that " man was created by the Trinity on 23d October, 4004 B. C., at nine oclock in the morning." The same theologian, who, by the way, was a very eminent Hebrew scholar, following the interpretation of the great Fathers of the Church, " declared, as the result of profound and exhaustive study of the Scriptures, that ' heaven and earth, centre and circumference, and clouds full of water, were created all together, in the same instant.' "

The story of the Deluge was held to furnish sufficing explanation of the organic remains yielded by the rocks, but failing this, a multitude of fantastic theories were at hand to explain the fossils. They were said to be due to a " formative quality " in the soil; to its " plastic virtue "; to a " lapidific juice "; to the " fermentation of fatty matter "; to " the influence of the heavenly bodies," or, as the late eminent naturalist, Philip Gosse, seriously suggested in his whimsical book Omphalos: an Attempt to untie the Geological Knot, they were but simulacra wherewith a mocking Deity rebuked the curiosity of man. Every explanation, save the right and obvious one, had its defenders, because it was essential to support some theory to rebut the evidence supplied by remains of animals as to the existence of death in the world before the fall of Adam. Otherwise, the statements in the Old Testament, on which the Pauline reasoning rested, were baseless, and to discredit these was to undermine the authority of the Scriptures from Genesis to the Apocalypse. No wonder, therefore, that theology was up in arms, or that it saw in geology a deadlier foe than astronomy had seemed to be in ages past. The Sorbonne, or Faculty of Theology, in Paris burnt the books of the geologists, banished their authors, and, in the case of Buffon, the famous naturalist, condemned him to retract the awful heresy, which was declared " contrary to the creed of the Church," contained in these words: " The waters of the sea have produced the mountains and valleys of the land; the waters of the heavens, reducing all to a level, will at last deliver the whole land over to the sea, and the sea successively prevailing over the land, will leave dry new continents like those which we inhabit." So the old man repeated the submission of Galileo, and published his recantation: "I declare that I had no intention to contradict the text of Scripture; that I believe most firmly all therein related about the creation, both as to order of time and matter of fact. I abandon everything in my book respecting the formation of the earth, and generally all which may be contrary to the narrative of Moses." That was in the year 1751.

If the English theologians could not deliver heretics of the type of Buffon to the secular arm, they used all the means that denunciation supplied for delivering them over to Satan. Epithets were hurled at them; arguments drawn from a world accursed of God levelled at them. Saint Jerome, living in the fourth century, had pointed to the cracked and crumpled rocks as proof of divine anger: now Wesley and others saw in "sin the moral cause of earthquakes, whatever their natural cause might be," since before Adam's transgression, no convulsions or eruptions ruffled the calm of Paradise. Meanwhile, the probing of the earth's crust went on; revealing, amidst all the seeming confusion of distorted and metamorphosed rocks, an unvarying sequence of strata, and of the fossils imbedded in them.

8

Different causes were assigned for the vast changes ranging over vast periods; one school believing in the action of volcanic and such like catastrophic agents; another in the action of aqueous agents, seeing, more consistently, in present operations the explanation of the causes of past changes. But there was no diversity of opinion concerning the extension of the earth's time-history and life-history to millions on millions of years.

So, when this was to be no longer resisted, theologians sought some basis of compromise on such non-fundamental points as the six days of creation. It was suggested that perhaps these did not mean the seventh part of a week, but periods, or eons, or something equally elastic; and that if the Mosaic narrative was regarded as a poetic revelation of the general succession of phenomena, beginning with the development of order out of chaos, and ending with the creation of man, Scripture would be found to have anticipated or revealed what science confirms. It was impossible, so theologians argued, that there could be aught else than harmony between the divine works and the writings which were assumed to be of divine origin. Science could not contradict revelation, and whatever seemed contradictory was due to misapprehension either of the natural fact, or to misreading of the written word. But although the story of the creation might be clothed, as so exalted and moving a theme warranted, in poetic form, that of the fall of Adam and of the drowning

of his descendants, eight persons excepted, must
be taken in all its appalling literalness. Confirmation
of the Deluge story was found in the fossil shells on
high mountain tops; while as for the giants of ante-
diluvian times, there were the huge bones in proof.
Some of these relics of mastodon and mammoth were
actually hung up in churches as evidence that " there
were giants in those days " ! Geoffroy Saint-Hilaire
tells of one Henrion, who published a book in 1718
giving the height of Adam as one hundred and
twenty-three feet nine inches, and of Eve as one hundred and eighteen feet nine inches, Noah being of
rather less stature. But to parley with science is
fatal to theology. Moreover, arguments which in-
volve the cause they support in ridicule may be left
to refute themselves. And while theology was hesitating, as in the amusing example supplied by Dr.
William Smith's Dictionary of the Bible (published
in 1863) wherein the reader, turning up the article " Deluge," is referred to " Flood," and thence
to " Noah " ; archæology produced the Chaldæan
original of the legend whence the story of the
flood is derived. With candour as commendable
as it is rare, the Reverend Professor Driver, from
whom quotation has been made already, admits
that " read without prejudice or bias, the narrative of Genesis i. creates an impression at variance with the facts revealed by science " ; all efforts at reconciliation being only " different modes
of obliterating the characteristic features of Gene-

sis, and of reading into it a view which it does not express."

While the ground in favour of the literal interpretation of Genesis was being contested, an invading force, that had been gathering strength with the years, was advancing in the shape of the science of Biology. The workers therein fall into two classes: the one, represented by Linnaeus and his school, applied themselves to the classifying and naming of plants and animals; the other, represented by Cuvier and his school, examined into structure and function. Anatomy made clear the machinery: physiology the work which it did, and the conditions under which the work was done. Then, through comparison of corresponding organs and their functions in various life-forms, came growing perception of their unity. But only to a few came gleams of that unity as proof of common descent of plant and animal, for, save in scattered hints of inter-relation between species, which occur from the time of Lord Bacon onward, the theory of their immutability was dominant until forty years ago.

Four men form the chief vanguard of the biological movement. ["Modern classificatory method and nomenclature have largely grown out of the work of Linnaeus; the modern conception of biology, as a science, and of its relation to climatology, geography, and geology, are as largely rooted in the labours of Buffon; comparative anatomy and palæontology owe a vast debt to Cuvier's results; while inverte-

brate zoology and the revival of the idea of Evolution are intimately dependent on the results of the
work of Lamarck. In other words, the main results
of biology up to the early years of this century are to
be found in, or spring out of, the works of these men."

Linnaeus, son of a Lutheran pastor, born at
Roeshult, in Sweden, in 1707, had barely passed his
twenty-fifth year before laying the ground-plan of
the system of classification which bears his name,
a system which advance in knowledge has since
modified. Based on external resemblances, its
formulation was possible only to a mind intent on
minute and accurate detail, and less observant of
general principles. In brief, the work of Linnaeus
was constructive, not interpretative. Hence, perhaps, conjoined to the theological ideas then current,
the reason why the larger question of the fixity of
species entered not into his purview. To him each
plant and animal retained the impress of the Creative
hand that had shaped it " in the beginning," and,
throughout his working life, he departed but slightly
from the plan with which he started, namely, " reckoning as many species as issued in pairs " from the
Almighty fiat.

Not so Buffon, born on his father's estate in Bur-
gundy in the same year as Linnaeus, whom he survived ten years, dying in 1788. His opinions, clash-
ing as they did with orthodox creeds, were given in
a tentative, questioning fashion, so that where ecclesiastical censure fell, retreat was easier. As has been

seen in his submission to the Sorbonne, he was not
of the stuff of which martyrs are made. Perhaps he
felt that the ultimate victory of his opinions was suf-
ficiently assured to make self-sacrifice needless. But,
under cover of pretence at inquiry, his convictions
are clear enough. He was no believer in the permanent stability of species, and noted, as warrant of
this, the otherwise unexplained presence of aborted
or rudimentary structures. For example, he says,
" the pig does not appear to have been formed upon
an original, special, and perfect plan, since it is a
compound of other animals; it has evidently useless
parts, or rather, parts of which it cannot make any
use, toes, all the bones of which are perfectly formed,
and which, nevertheless, are of no service to it. Nature is far from subjecting herself to final causes in
the formation of her creatures." Then, further, as
showing his convictions on the non-fixity of species,
he says, how many of them, " being perfected or de-
generated by the great changes in land and sea, by
the favours or disfavours of Nature, by food, by the
prolonged influences of climate, contrary or favourable, are no longer what they formerly were." But
he writes with an eye on the Sorbonne when, hinting
at a possible common ancestor of horse and ass, and
of ape and man, he slyly adds that since the Bible
teaches the contrary, the thing cannot be. Thus he
attacked covertly; by adit, not by direct assault;
and to those who read between the lines there was
given a key wherewith to unlock the door to the

solution of many biological problems. Buffon, consequently, was the most stimulating and suggestive
naturalist of the eighteenth century. There comes
between him and Lamarck, both in order of time
and sequence of ideas, Erasmus Darwin, the distinguished grandfather of Charles Darwin.

Born at Eton, near Newark, in 1731, he walked
the hospitals at London and Edinburgh, and settled,
for some years, at Lichfield, ultimately removing to
Derby. Since Lucretius, no scientific writer had
put his cosmogonic speculations into verse until Dr.
Darwin made the heroic metre, in which stereotyped
form the poetry of his time was cast, the vehicle of
rhetorical descriptions of the amours of flowers and
the evolution of the thumb. The Loves of the Plants,
ridiculed in the Loves of the Triangles in the Anti-
Jacobin, is not to be named in the same breath, for
stateliness of diction, and majesty of movement, as
the De rerum Natura. But both the prose work
Zoonomia and the poem The Temple of Nature (published after the author's death in 1802) have claim
to notice as the matured expression of conclusions at
which the clear-sighted, thoughtful, and withal, eccentric doctor had arrived in the closing years of his
life. Krause's Life and Study of the Works of Erasmus Darwin supplies an excellent outline of the contents of books which are now rarely taken down
from the shelves, and makes clear that their author
had the root of the matter in him. His observations
and reading, for the influence of Buffon and others

is apparent in his writings, led him to reject the current belief in the separate creation of species. He saw that this theory wholly failed to account for the existence of abnormal forms, of adaptations of the structure of organs to their work, of gradations between living things, and other features inconsistent with the doctrine of " let lions be, and there were lions." His shrewd comment on the preformation notion of development has been quoted (p. 20). The substance of his argument in support of a " physical basis of life " is as follows: " When we revolve in our minds the metamorphosis of animals, as from the tadpole to the frog; secondly, the changes produced by artificial cultivation, as in the breeds of horses, dogs, and sheep; thirdly, the changes produced by conditions of climate and of season, as in the sheep of warm climates being covered with hair instead of wool, and the hares and partridges of northern climates becoming white in winter; when, further, we observe the changes of structure produced by habit, as seen especially by men of different occupations; or the changes produced by artificial mutilation and prenatal influences, as in the crossing of species and production of monsters; fourth, when we observe the essential unity of plan in all warm-blooded animals—we are led to conclude that they have been alike produced from a similar living filament." The concluding words of this extract make remarkable approach to the modern theory of the origin of life in the complex jelly-

like protoplasm, or, as some call it, nuclein or nucleo-
plasm. And, on this, Erasmus Darwin further remarks: "As the earth and ocean were probably
peopled with vegetable productions long before the
existence of animals, and many families of these
animals long before other animals of them, shall we
conjecture that one and the same kind of living filament is and has been the cause of all organic life?"
Nor does he make any exception to this law of organic development. He quotes Buffon and Hel-
vetius to the effect—"that many features in the anatomy of man point to a former quadrupedal position,
and indicate that he is not yet fully adapted to the
erect position; that, further, man may have arisen
from a single family of monkeys, in which, accidentally, the opposing muscle brought the thumb against
the tips of the fingers, and that this muscle gradually
increased in size by use in successive generations."
While we who live in these days of fuller knowledge
of agents of variation may detect the *minus* in all
foregoing speculations, our interest is increased in
the thought of their near approach to the cardinal
discovery. And a rapid run through the later writings of Dr. Darwin shows that there is scarcely a
side of the great theory of Evolution which has escaped his notice or suggestive comment. Grant
Allen, in his excellent little monograph on Charles
Darwin, says that the theory of "natural selection
was the only cardinal one in the evolutionary system
on which Erasmus Darwin did not actually forestall

his more famous and greater namesake. For its full perception, the discovery of Malthus had to be collated with the speculations of Buffon."

In the Historical Sketch on the Progress of Opinion on the Origin of Species, which Darwin prefixed to his book, he refers to Lamarck as " the first man whose conclusions on the subject excited much attention; " rendering " the eminent service of arousing attention to the probability of all change in the organic, as well as in the inorganic world, being the result of law, and not of miraculous inter-position." Lamarck was born at Bezantin, in Picardy, in 1744. Intended for the Church, he chose the army, but an injury resulting from a practical joke cut short his career as a soldier. He then became a banker's clerk, in which occupation he secured leisure for his favourite pursuit of natural history. Through Buffon's influence he procured a civil appointment, and ultimately became a colleague of Cuvier and Geoffroy St. Hilaire in the Museum of Natural History at Paris. Of Cuvier it will here suffice to say that he remained to the end of his life a believer in special creation, or, what amounts to the same thing, a series of special creations which, he held, followed the catastrophic annihilations of prior plants and animals. Although orthodox by conviction, his researches told against his tenets, because his important work in the reconstruction of skeletons of long extinct animals laid the foundation of palæontology.

To Lamarck, says Haeckel, " will always belong
the immortal glory of having for the first time worked
out the Theory of Descent as an independent scientific theory of the first order, and as the philosophical foundation of the whole science of Biology." He
taught that in the beginnings of life only the very simplest and lowest animals and plants came into existence; those of more complex structure developing
from these; man himself being descended from ape-
like mammals. For the Aristotelian mechanical figure
of life as a ladder, with its detached steps, he substituted
the more appropriate figure of a tree, as an inter-
related organism. He argued that the course of the
earth's development, and also of all life upon it, was
continuous, and not interrupted by violent revolutions. In this he followed Buffon and Hutton. Buffon, in his Theory of the Earth, argues that " in
order to understand what had taken place in the past,
or what will happen in the future, we have but to
observe what is going on in the present." This is
the keynote of modern geology. " Life," adds
Lamarck, " is a purely physical phenomenon. All
its phenomena depend on mechanical, physical, and
chemical causes which are inherent in the nature of
matter itself." He believed in a form of spontaneous
generation. Rejecting Buffon's theory of the direct
action of the surroundings as agents of change in
living things, he sums up the causes of organic evolution in the following propositions:

1. Life tends by its inherent forces to increase

the volume of each living body and of all its parts up to a limit determined by its own needs.

2. New wants in animals give rise to new movements which produce organs.

3. The development of these organs is in proportion to their employment.

4. New developments are transmitted to offspring.

The second and third propositions were illustrated by examples which have, with good reason, provoked ridicule. Lamarck accounts for the long neck of the giraffe by that organ being continually stretched out to reach the leaves at the tree-tops; for the long tongue of the ant-eater or the woodpecker by these creatures protruding it to get at food in channel or crevice; for the webbed feet of aquatic animals by the outstretching of the membranes between the toes in swimming; and for the erect position of man by the constant efforts of his ape-like ancestors to keep upright. The legless condition of the serpent which, in the legend of the Garden of Eden, is accounted for on moral grounds, is thus explained by Lamarck: "Snakes sprang from reptiles with four extremities, but having taken up the habit of moving along the earth and concealing themselves among bushes, their bodies, owing to repeated efforts to elongate themselves and to pass through narrow spaces, have acquired a considerable length out of all proportion to their width. Since long feet would have been very useless, and short feet would have been incapable of moving their bodies, there resulted a cessation of use of these parts, which has finally caused them to totally disappear, although they were originally part of the plan of organization in these animals." The discovery of an efficient cause of modifications, which Lamarck refers to the efforts of the creatures themselves, has placed his speculations in the museum of biological curiosities; but sharp controversy rages to-day over the question raised in Lamarck's fourth proposition, namely, the transmission of characters acquired by the parent during its lifetime to the offspring. This burning question between Weismann and his opponents, involving the serious problem of heredity, will remain unsettled till a long series of observations supply material for judgment.

Lamarck, poor, neglected, and blind in his old age, died in 1829. Both Cuvier, who ridiculed him, and Goethe, who never heard of him, passed away three years later. The year following his death, when Darwin was an undergraduate at Cambridge, Lyell published his Principles of Geology, a work destined to assist in paving the way for the removal of one difficulty attending the solution of the theory of the origin of species, namely, the vast period of time for the life-history of the globe which that theory demands. As Lyell, however, was then a believer—although, like a few others of his time, of wavering type—in the fixity of species, he had other aims in view than those to which his book contributed. But

he wrote with an open mind, not being, as Herbert
Spencer says of Hugh Miller, " a theologian studying geology." Following the theories of uniformity
of action laid down by Hutton, by Buffon, and by
that industrious surveyor, William Smith, who travelled the length and breadth of England, mapping
out the sequence of the rocks, and tabulating the
fossils special to each stratum, Lyell demonstrated
in detail that the formation and features of the earth's
crust are explained by the operation of causes still
active. He was one among others, each working
independently at different branches of research;
each, unwittingly, collecting evidence which would
help to demolish old ideas, and support new theories.

A year after the Principles of Geology appeared,
there crept unnoticed into the world a treatise, by
one Patrick Matthew, on Naval Timber and Arboriculture, under which unexciting title Darwin's theory
was anticipated. Of this, however, as of a still earlier
anticipation, more presently. About this period Von
Baer, in examining the embryos of animals, showed
that creatures so unlike one another in their adult
state as fishes, lizards, lions, and men, resemble one
another so closely in the earlier stages of their development that no differences can be detected between them. But Von Baer was himself anticipated
by Meckel, who wrote as follows in 1811: " There is
no good physiologist who has not been struck, in-
cidentally, by the observation that the original form
of all organisms is one and the same, and that out

of this one form, all, the lowest as well as the highest, are developed in such a manner that the latter pass through the permanent forms of the former as transitory stages" (Osborn's From the Greeks to Darwin, p. 212). In botany Conrad Sprengel, who belongs to the eighteenth century, had shown the work effected by insects in the fertilization of plants. Following his researches, Robert Brown made clear the mode of the development of plants, and Sir William Hooker traced their habits and geographical distribution. Von Mohl discovered that material basis of both plant and animal which he named " protoplasm." In 1844, nine years before Von Mohl told the story of the building-up of life from a seemingly structureless jelly, a book appeared which critics of the time charged with " poisoning the fountains of science, and sapping the foundations of religion." This was the once famous Vestiges of Creation, acknowledged after his death as the work of Robert Chambers, in which the origin and movements of the solar system were explained as determined by uniform laws, themselves the expression of Divine power. Organisms, " from the simplest and oldest, up to the highest and most recent," were the result of an " inherent impulse imparted by the Almighty both to advance them from the several grades and modify their structure as circumstances required." Although now referred to only as " marking time " in the history of the theory of Evolution, the book created a sensation which died away only some years after its publication. Darwin remarks upon it in his Historical Sketch that although displaying " in the earlier editions little accurate knowledge and a great want of scientific knowledge, it did excellent service in this country in calling attention to the subject, in removing prejudice, and in thus preparing the ground for the reception of analogous views."

Three years after the Vestiges, there was, although none then knew it, or knowing the fact, would have admitted it, more " sapping of the foundations " of orthodox belief, when M. Boucher de Perthes exhibited some rudely-shaped flint implements which had been found at intervals in hitherto undisturbed deposits of sand and gravel—old river beds—in the Somme valley, near Abbeville, in Picardy. For these rough stone tools and weapons, being of human workmanship, evidenced the existence of savage races of men in Europe in a dim and dateless past, and went far to refute the theories of his paradisiacal state on that memorable " 23 October, 4004 B. C.," when, according to Dr. Lightfoot's reckoning (see p. 95), Adam was created. While the pickaxe, in disturbing flint knives and spearheads, that had lain for countless ages, was disturbing much besides, English and German philosophers were formulating the imposing theory which, under the name of the Conservation of Energy, makes clear the indestructibility of both matter and motion. Then, to complete the work of preparation effected by the discoveries now briefly outlined, there appeared, in a

now defunct newspaper, the Leader, in its issue of
20th of March, 1852, an article by Herbert Spencer
on the Development Hypothesis, in which the following striking passage occurs: "Those who cava-
lierly reject the Theory of Evolution, as not ade-
quately supported by facts, seem quite to forget that
their own theory is supported by no facts at all. Like
the majority of men who are born to a given belief,
they demand the most rigorous proof of any adverse
belief, but assume that their own needs none. Here
we find, scattered over the globe, vegetable and animal organisms numbering, of the one kind (according to Humboldt) some 320,000 species, and of the
other, some 2,000,000 species (see Carpenter); and
if to these we add the numbers of animal and vegetable species that have become extinct, we may safely
estimate the number of species that have existed,
and are existing, on the earth, at not less than *ten
millions.* Well, which is the most rational theory
about these ten millions of species? Is it most likely
that there have been ten millions of special creations?
or is it most likely that by continual modifications,
due to change of circumstances, ten millions of varieties have been produced, as varieties are being produced still? . . . Even could the supporters of the
Development Hypothesis merely show that the origi-
nation of species by the process of modification is
conceivable, they would be in a better position than
their opponents. But they can do much more than
this. They can show that the process of modification

9

has effected, and is effecting, decided changes in all organisms subject to modifying influences. . . . They can show that in successive generations these changes continue, until ultimately the new conditions become the natural ones. They can show that in cultivated plants, domesticated animals, and in the several races of men, such alterations have taken place. They can show that the degrees of difference so produced are often, as in dogs, greater than those on which distinctions of species are in other cases founded. They can show, too, that the changes daily taking place in ourselves—the facility that attends long practice, and the loss of aptitude that begins when practice ceases—the strengthening of passions habitually gratified, and the weakening of those habitually curbed—the development of every faculty, bodily, moral, or intellectual, according to the use made of it—are all explicable on this same principle. And thus they can show that throughout all organic nature there *is* at work a modifying influence of the kind they assign as the cause of these specific differences; an influence which, though slow in its action, does, in time, if the circumstances demand it, produce marked changes—an influence which, to all appearance, would produce in the millions of years, and under the great varieties of condition which geological records imply, any amount of change."

This quotation shows, as perhaps no other reference might show, how, by the middle of the present century, science was trembling on the verge of dis-

covery of that " modifying influence " of which Mr.
Spencer speaks. That discovery made clear how all
that had preceded it not only contributed thereto, but
gained a significance and value which, apart from it,
could not have been secured. When the relation of
the several parts to the whole became manifest, each
fell into its place like the pieces of a child's puzzle
map.

LEADING MEN OF SCIENCE.

A. D. 800 TO A. D. 1800.

NAME.	Place and date of birth.	Died.	Speciality.
Geber (Djafer).	Mesopotamia, 830.	....	Earliest known Chemist.
Avicenna (Ibu Sina).	Bokhara, 980.	1037	Expositor of Aristotle; Physician and Geologist.
Averroes (Ibu Roshd).	Spain, 1126.	1198	Translator and Commentator of Aristotle.
Roger Bacon.	Ilchester, 1214.	1292	First English Experimentalist.
Christopher Columbus.	Genoa, 1445.	1506	Discoverer of America, 1492.
Vasco de Gama.	Sines, 1469. (Portugal.)	1525	Sailed round the South of Africa, 1497.
Ferdinand Magellan.	Ville de Sabroza, 1470.	1521	Circumnavigator of the Globe, 1519.
Nicholas Copernicus.	Thorn, 1473. (Prussia.)	1543	Discoverer of the Sun as the Centre of our System.
Andreas Vesalius.	Brussels, 1514.	1564	Human Anatomist.
Conrad Gesner.	Zurich, 1516.	1565	Classification of Plants and Animals.
Andrew Caesalpino.	Arezzo, 1519. (Tuscany.)	1603	Comparative Botanist.
Tycho Brahe.	Knudstrup, 1546. (Sweden.)	1601	Collector of Astronomical Data.

Name.	Place and date of birth.	Died.	Speciality.
Giordano Bruno.	Nola, 1550.	1600	Expounder of the Copernican System and Philosopher.
Francis, Lord Bacon.	London, 1561.	1626	Expounder of the Inductive Philosophy.
Galileo Galilei.	Pisa, 1564.	1642	Numerous Astronomical Discoveries.
Johann Kepler.	Würtemburg, 1571.	1630	Discoverer of the Three Laws of Planetary Movements.
Thomas Hobbes.	Malmesbury, 1588.	1679	One of the Founders of Modern Ethics.
Renè Descartes.	La Haye, 1596. (Touraine.)	1650	Resolution of all Phenomena into Terms of Matter and Motion. (Dualism.)
Benedict Spinoza.	Amsterdam, 1632.	1677	Resolution of all Phenomena into Terms of Substance=God. (Monism.)
John Locke.	Wrington, 1632. (Somerset.)	1704	Moral Philosopher.
Gottfrid Wilhelm Leibnitz.	Leipsic, 1646.	1716	Philosopher and Mathematician.
Sir Isaac Newton.	Woolsthorpe, 1642. (Lincoln.)	1727	Expounder of the Law of Gravitation.
Edmund Halley.	London, 1656.	1741	Astronomer.
David Hartley.	Illingworth, 1705.	1757	Psychology of Man.
Carl von Linnaeus.	Roeshult, 1707. (Sweden.)	1778	Systematic Botany and Zoology.
Count de Buffon.	Burgundy, 1707.	1788	Contributions from Biology toward Theory of Evolution and Geology.
David Hume.	Edinburgh, 1711.	1776	Philosophy of the Anti-supernatural ; all Science Converging in Man.
Immanuel Kant.	Königsberg, 1724.	1804	Formulator of the Nebular Theory.
James Hutton.	Edinburgh, 1726.	1797	Geologist : Uniformitarian.

Name.	Place and date of birth.	Died.	Speciality.
Erasmus Darwin.	Elton, 1731. (Lincolnshire.)	1802	(*See* Buffon.)
Sir William Herschel.	Hanover, 1738.	1822	Astronomer.
Jean Baptiste Lamarck.	Bazantium, 1744.	1829	Biologist : Contributions against fixity of Species.
Marquis de Laplace.	Beaumont-en-Ange, 1749.	1827	Expounder of the Nebular Theory.
Conrad Sprengel.	Pomerania, 1766.	1833	Botanist.
John Dalton.	Eaglesfield, 1767. (Cumberland.)	1844	Formulator of the Modern Atomic Theory.
Baron Cuvier.	Montbeliard, 1769.	1832	Palæontologist and Anatomist.
Geoff. St. Hilaire.	Etampes, 1772.	1844	Zoologist.
Alexander von Humboldt.	Berlin, 1769.	1859	Explorer.
William Smith.	Churchill, 1769. (Oxon.)	1840	Geologist : mapped Strata of Great Britain.
Boucher de Perthes.	1788.	1868	Discoverer of Evidences of Man's Antiquity.
Sir William Hooker.	Norwich, 1785.	1865	Botanist.
Sir Charles Lyell.	Kinnordy, 1797. (Forfarshire.)	1875	Geologist : developed Hutton's Theory.
Ernst von Baer.	Esthonia, 1792.	1876	Embryologist: Law of Organic Development.
Sir Richard Owen.	Lancaster, 1804.	1892	Palæontologist.
Hugo von Mohl.	Germany, 1805.	1872	Discoverer of Protoplasm.
Theodor Schwann.	Neuss, 1810. (Prussia.)	1882	Founder of the Cell Theory.
Hermann von Helmholtz.	Potsdam, 1821.	1894	Formulator of the Doctrine of the Conservation of Energy.

PART IV.

MODERN EVOLUTION.

1. *Darwin and Wallace.*

We have to deal with Man as a product of Evolution ; with Society as a product of Evolution ; and with Moral Phenomena as products of Evolution.—HERBERT SPENCER, Principles of Ethics, § 193.

CHARLES ROBERT DARWIN (the second name was rarely used by him) was born at Shrewsbury on the 12th of February, 1809. He came of a long line of Lincolnshire yeomen, whose forbears spelt the name variously, as Darwen, Derwent, and Darwynne, perhaps deriving it from the river of kindred name. His father was a kindly, prosperous doctor, of sufficient scientific reputation to secure his election into the Royal Society, although that coveted honour was then more easily obtained than now. Of the more famous grandfather, Erasmus Darwin, the reminder suffices that both his prose and poetry were vehicles of suggestive speculations on the development of life-forms. Dealing with bald facts and dates for clearance of what follows, it may be added that Charles Darwin was educated at the Grammar School of his native town; that he passed thence to Edinburgh and Cambridge Universities; was occupied as volunteer naturalist on board the Beagle from

Photo. by London. Stereoscopic C⁰

Alfred R. Wallace

December, 1831, till October, 1836; that he published his epoch-making Origin of Species in November, 1859; and that he was buried by the side of Sir Isaac Newton in Westminster Abbey on the 26th of April, 1882.

As with not a few other men of " light and leading," neither school nor university did much for him, nor did his boyhood give indication of future greatness. In his answers to the series of questions addressed to various scientific men in 1873 by his distinguished cousin, Francis Galton, he says: " I consider that all I have learnt of any value has been self-taught," and he adds that his education fostered no methods of observation or reasoning. Of the Shrewsbury Grammar School, where, after the death of his mother (daughter of Josiah Wedgwood, the celebrated potter), in his ninth year, he was placed as a boarder till his sixteenth year, he tells us, in the modest and candid Autobiography printed in the Life and Letters, " nothing could have been worse for the development of my mind." All that he was taught were the classics, and a little ancient geography and history; no mathematics, and no modern languages. Happily, he had inherited a taste for natural history and for collecting, his spoils including not only shells and plants, but also coins and seals. When the fact that he helped his brother in chemical experiments became known to Dr. Butler, the head-master, that desiccated pedagogue publicly rebuked him " for wasting time on such useless subjects." Then his father, angry at finding that he was doing no good at school, reproved him for caring for nothing but shooting, dogs, and rat-catching, and declared that he would be a disgrace to the family! He sent him to Edinburgh University with his brother to study medicine, but Darwin found the dulness of the lectures intolerable, and the sight of blood sickened him, as it did his father. Although the effect of the " incredibly " dry lectures on geology made him—the future Secretary of the Geological Society!—vow never to read a book on the science, or in any way study it, his interest in biological subjects grew, and its first fruits were shown in a paper read before the Plinian Society at Edinburgh in 1826, in which he reported his discovery that the so-called ova of *Flustra*, or the sea-mat, were larvæ.

But his father had to accept the fact that Darwin disliked the idea of being a doctor, and fearing that he would degenerate into an idle sporting man, proposed that he should become a clergyman! Darwin says upon this:—

I asked for some time to consider, as from what little I had heard or thought on the subject I had scruples about declaring my belief in all the dogmas of the Church of England, though otherwise I liked the thought of being a country clergyman. Accordingly I read with care Pearson on the Creed, and a few other books on divinity; and, as I did not then in the least doubt the strict and literal truth of every word in the Bible, I soon persuaded myself that our creed must be fully accepted. Considering how fiercely I have been attacked by the orthodox, it seems ludicrous that I once intended to be a clergyman. Nor was this intention and my father's wish ever formally given up, but died a natural death when, on leaving Cambridge, I joined the Beagle as naturalist. If the phrenologists are to be trusted, I was well fitted in one respect to be a clergyman. A few years ago the secretaries of a German psychological society asked me earnestly by letter for a photograph of myself ; and some time afterwards I received the proceedings of one of the meetings, in which it seemed that the shape of my head had been the subject of a public discussion, and one of the speakers declared that I had the bump of reverence developed enough for ten priests.

The result was that early in 1828 Darwin went to Cambridge, the three years spent at which were "time wasted, as far as the academical studies were concerned." His passion for shooting and hunting led him into a sporting, card-playing, drinking company, but science was his redemption. No pursuit gave him so much pleasure as collecting beetles, of his zeal in which the following is an example: "One day, on tearing off some old bark, I saw two rare beetles, and seized one in each hand; then I saw a third and new kind, which I could not bear to lose, so I popped the one which I held in my right hand into my mouth. Alas! it ejected some intensely acrid fluid, which burnt my tongue so that I was forced to spit the beetle out, which was lost, as was the third one."

Happily for his future career, and therefore for the interests of science, Darwin became intimate with men like Whewell, Henslow, and Sedgwick, while the reading of Humboldt's Personal Narrative, and of Sir John Herschel's Introduction to Natural Philosophy, stirred up in him " a burning zeal to add even the most humble contribution to the noble structure of Natural Science." The vow to eschew geology was quickly broken when he came under the spell of Sedgwick's influence, but it was the friendship of Henslow that determined his after career, and prevented him from becoming the " Rev. Charles Darwin." For on his return from a geological tour in Wales with Sedgwick he found a letter from Henslow awaiting him, the purport of which is in the following extract:—

"I have been asked by Peacock (Lowndean Professor of Astronomy at Cambridge) to recommend him a naturalist as companion to Captain Fitz-Roy, employed by Government to survey the southern extremity of America. I have stated that I consider you to be the best-qualified person I know of who is likely to undertake such a situation."

In connection with this the following memorandum from Darwin's pocket-book of 1831 is of interest:—" Returned to Shrewsbury at end of August. Refused offer of voyage."

This refusal was given at the instance of his father, who objected to the scheme as "wild and unsettling, and as disreputable to his character as a clergyman"; but he soon yielded on the advice of his brother-in-law, Josiah Wedgwood, and on Darwin's plea that he " should be deuced clever to spend more than his allowance whilst on board the Beagle." On this his father answered with a smile, " But they

tell me you are very clever." It is amusing to find
that Darwin narrowly escaped being rejected by
Fitz-Roy, who, as a disciple of Lavater, doubted
whether a man with such a nose as Darwin's " could
possess sufficient energy and determination for the
voyage."

The details of that voyage, the first of the two
memorable events in Darwin's otherwise unadventur-
ous life, are set down in delightful narrative in his
Naturalist's Voyage Round the World, and it will
suffice to quote a passage from the autobiography
bearing on the significance of the materials collected
during his five years' absence.

During the voyage of the Beagle I had been deeply impressed by discovering in the Pampean formation great fossil
animals covered with armour like that on the existing arma-
dillos; secondly, by the manner in which closely allied animals
replace one another in proceeding southwards over the continent; and thirdly, by the South American character of most
of the productions of the Galapagos Archipelago, and more
especially by the manner in which they differ slightly on each
island of the group, none of the islands appearing to be very
ancient in a geological sense. It was evident that such facts
as these, as well as many others, could only be explained on
the supposition that species gradually became modified; and
the subject haunted me. But it was equally evident that
"none of the evolutionary theories then current in the scientific world" could account for the innumerable cases in which
organisms of every kind are beautifully adapted to their habits
of life. . . . I had always been much struck by such adaptations, and until these could be explained, it seemed to me
almost useless to endeavour to prove by indirect evidence that
species have been modified. . . . In October, 1838, that is,

fifteen months after I had begun my systematic inquiry, I happened to read for amusement Malthus on Population, and being well prepared to appreciate the struggle for existence which everywhere goes on, from long-continued observations of the habits of plants and animals, it at once struck me that under these circumstances favourable variations would tend to be preserved, and unfavourable ones destroyed. The result of this would be the formation of new species.

Shortly after his return he settled in London, prepared his journal and manuscripts of observations for publication, and opened, he says, under date of July, 1837, " my first note-book for facts in relation to the origin of species, about which I had long reflected, and never ceased working for the next twenty years." He acted for two years as one of the honorary secretaries of the Geological Society, which brought him into close relations with Lyell, and, as his health then allowed him to go into society, he saw a good deal of prominent literary and scientific contemporaries.

In the autumn of 1842, two years and eight months after his marriage with his first cousin, Emma Wedgwood, who died in October last (1896), Darwin removed from London, the air and social demands of which were alike unsuited to his health, and finally fixed upon a house in the secluded village of Down, near Beckenham, where he spent the rest of his days. Henceforth the life of Darwin is merged in the books in which, from time to time, he gave the result of his long years of patient observation and inquiry, from the epoch-making Origin to the monograph on earthworms. With bad health, apparently due to gouty tendencies aggravated by chronic sea-sickness during his voyage; with nights that never gave unbroken sleep; and days that were never passed without prostrating pain; he might well have felt justified in doing nothing whatever. But he was saved from the accursed monotony of a wealthy invalid's life by his insatiate delight in searching for that solution of the problem of the mutability of species which time would not fail to bring. In this, he tells us, he forgot his "daily discomfort," and thus was delivered from morbid introspection.

Darwin worked at his rough notes on the variation of animals and plants under domestication, adding facts collected by "printed enquiries, by conversations with skilful breeders and gardeners, and by extensive reading," gleams of light coming till he says that he is "almost convinced that species are not (it is like confessing a murder) immutable." But he was still groping in the dark as to the application of selection to wild plants and animals, until, as remarked above, the chance reading of Malthus suggested a working theory. A brief sketch of this theory, written out in pencil in 1842, was elaborated in 1844 into an essay of two hundred and thirty pages. The importance attached to this was shown in a letter which Darwin then addressed to his wife, charging her, in the event of his death, to apply £400 to the expense of publication. He also named

certain competent men from whom an editor might
be chosen, preference being given to Sir Charles
(then Mr. Lyell, at whose advice Darwin began to
write out his views on a scale three or four times as
extensive as that in which they appeared in the
Origin of Species. Their publication in an abstract
form was hastened by the receipt, in June, 1858, of
a paper, containing " exactly the same theory," from
Mr. Alfred Russel Wallace at Ternate in the
Moluccas. This reference to that distinguished explorer, will, before the story of the coincident discovery is further told, fitly introduce a sketch of his
career.

ALFRED RUSSEL WALLACE was born at Usk, in
Monmouthshire, on the 8th of January, 1823. He was
educated at Hereford Grammar School, and in his
fourteenth year began the study of land-surveying
and architecture under an elder brother. Quick-
witted and observing, he studied a great deal more
on his own account in his journeyings over England
and Wales, the results of which abide in the wide
range of subjects—scientific, political, and social—
engaging his active pen from early manhood to the
present day.

About 1844 he exchanged the theodolite for the
ferule, and became English master in the Collegiate
School at Leicester, in which town he found a con-
genial friend in the person of his future fellow-trav-
eller, Henry Walter Bates. Bates was then employed
in his father's hosiery warehouse, from which he

escaped, as often as the long working hours then prevailing allowed, into the fields with his collecting-box. Both schoolmaster and shopman were ardent naturalists, Mr. Wallace, as he tells us, being at that time " chiefly interested in botany," but he afterward took up his friend's favourite pursuit of entomology. The writer, when preparing his memoir of Bates (which prefaces a reprint of the first edition of the delightful Naturalist on the Amazons), learned from Mr. Wallace that in early life he did not keep letters from Bates and other correspondents. But, fortunately, among Bates's papers, there was a bundle of interesting letters from Wallace written between June, 1845, and October, 1847, from Neath, in South Wales, to which town he had removed. In one of these, dated the 9th of November, 1845, Wallace asks Bates if he had read the Vestiges of the Natural History of Creation, and a subsequent letter indicates that Bates had not formed a favourable opinion of the book. A later letter is interesting as conveying an estimate of Darwin. " I first," Wallace says, " read Darwin's Journal three or four years back, and have lately re-read it. As the journal of a scientific traveller, it is second only to Humboldt's Personal Narrative; as a work of general interest, perhaps superor to it. He is an ardent admirer and most able supporter of Mr. Lyell's views. His style of writing I very much admire, so free from all labour, affectation, or egotism, yet so full of interest and original thought."

But, of still greater moment, is a letter in which Wallace tells Bates that he begins " to feel dissatisfied with a mere local collection.   I should like to take some one family to study thoroughly, principally with a view to the theory of the origin of species."   The two friends had often discussed schemes for going abroad to explore some virgin region, nor could their scanty means prevent the fulfilment of a scheme which has enriched both science and the literature of travel.   The choice of country to explore was settled by Wallace's perusal of a little book entitled A Voyage up the River Amazons, including a Residence in Pará, by W. H. Edwards, an American tourist, published in Murray's Family Library, in 1847.   In the autumn of that year Wallace proposed a joint expedition to the river Amazons for the purpose of exploring the Natural History of its banks; the plan being to make a collection of objects, dispose of the duplicates in London to pay expenses, and gather facts, as Mr. Wallace expressed it in one of his letters, "towards solving the problem of the origin of species."

The choice was a happy one, for, except by the German zoologist Von Spix, and the botanist Von Martius in 1817-20, and subsequently by Count de Castelnau, no exploration of a region so rich and interesting to the biologist had been attempted. Early in 1848 Bates and Wallace met in London to study South American animals and plants in the principal collections, and afterward went to Chatsworth to gain information about orchids, which they proposed to collect in the moist tropical forests and send home.

On 26th of April, 1848, they embarked at Liverpool in a barque of only 192 tons burden, one of the few ships then trading to Pará, to which seaport of the Amazons region a swift passage, "straight as an arrow," brought them on 28th of May.

The travellers soon settled in a *rocinha*, or country-house, a mile and half from Pará, and close to the forest, which came down to their doors. Like other towns along the Amazons, Pará stands on ground cleared from the forest that stretches, a wellnigh pathless jungle of luxuriant primeval vegetation, two thousand miles inland. In that paradise of the naturalist, the collectors gathered consignments which met with ready sale in London, and thus spent a couple of years in pursuits moderately remunerative and wholly pleasurable, till, on reaching Barra, at the mouth of the Rio Negro, one thousand miles from Pará, in March, 1850, Bates and Wallace, who was accompanied by his younger brother, parted company, "finding it more convenient to explore separate districts and collect independently." Wallace took the northern parts and tributaries of the Amazons, and Bates kept to the main stream, which, from the direction it seems to take at the fork of the Rio Negro, is called the Upper Amazons or the Solimoens. Different in character

10

and climatic conditions from the Lower Amazons, it flows through a " vast plain about a thousand miles in length, and five hundred or six hundred miles in breadth covered with one uniform, lofty, impervious, and humid forest." Bates stayed in the country till June, 1859, but Wallace left in 1852, and in the following year published an account of his journey under the title of Travels on the Amazon and Rio Negro. That book was written under the serious disadvantage of the destruction of the greater part of the notes and specimens by the burning of the ship in which Mr. Wallace took passage on his home-ward voyage. That it remains one of the select company of works of travel for which demand is continuous is evidenced in a reprint which appeared in 1891. If it affords few hints of the author's bent of mind toward the question of the origin of species, it shows what interest was being aroused within him over the allied subject of the geographical distribution of plants and animals which Mr. Wallace was to make so markedly his own.

In 1854 he sailed for the Malay Archipelago, where nearly eight years were spent in exploring the region from Sumatra to New Guinea. The large and varied outcome of that labour was embodied in numerous papers communicated to learned societies and scientific journals, and in a series of delightful books from The Malay Archipelago, first published in 1869, to Island Life, published in 1880. Among the minor results of his extensive travels—for all else that Wallace did pales before the great discovery which links his name with Darwin's—was the establishment of a line, known as "Wallace's," which divides the Malay Archipelago into two main groups, "Indo-Malaysia and Austro-Malaysia, marked by distinct species and groups of animals." That line runs through a deep channel separating the islands of Bali and Lombok; the plants and animals on which, although but fifteen miles of water separate them, differ from each other even more than do the islands of Great Britain and Japan. "A similar line, but somewhat farther east, divides on the whole the Malay from the Papuan races of man."

Among the more fugitive contributions which mark Mr. Wallace's approach to a solution of the problem in quest of which he and Bates went to the Amazons is a paper On the Law which has Regulated the Introduction of New Species, published in the Annals and Magazine of Natural History, 1855. In this he shows that some form of evolution of one species from another is needed to explain the geological and geographical facts of which examples are given.

In the interesting preface to the reprint of the famous paper On the Tendencies of Varieties to depart Indefinitely from the Original Type, Mr. Wallace recites the several researches which he made in quest of that "form" till, when lying ill with fever at Ternate, in February, 1858, something led him to think of the "positive checks" described by Malthus in his Essay on Population, a book which he had read some years before. Oddly enough, therefore, the honours lie with the maligned Haileybury Reverend Professor of Political Economy in furnishing both Darwin and Wallace with the clue. The " positive checks "—war, disease, famine—Wallace felt must act even more effectively on the lower animals than on man, because of their more rapid rate of multiplication. And he tells us, in the prefatory note to a reprint of his paper, " there suddenly flashed on me the *idea* of the survival of the fittest, and in the two hours that elapsed before my ague fit was over I had thought out the whole of the theory, and in the two succeeding evenings wrote it out in full and sent it by the next post to Mr. Darwin," asking him, if he thought well of the essay, to send it to Lyell. This Darwin did with the following remarks: " Your words have come true with a vengeance—that I should be forestalled. . . . I never saw a more striking coincidence; if Wallace had my MS. sketch written out in 1842, he could not have made a better short abstract! Even his terms now stand as heads of my chapters. Please return me the MS., which he does not say he wishes me to publish; but I shall, of course, at once write and offer to send to any journal. So all my originality, whatever it may amount to, will be smashed, though my book, if it will ever have any value, will not be deteriorated, as all the labour consists in the application of the theory." Darwin came out well in this business.

For to have hit upon a theory which interprets so large a question as the origin and causes of modification of life-forms; to keep on turning it over and over again in the mind for twenty long years; to spend the working hours of every day in collection and verification of facts for and against it; and then to have another man launching a " bolt from .the blue " in the shape of a paper with exactly the same theory, might well disturb even a philosopher of Darwin's serenity.

However, both Hooker and Lyell had read his sketch a dozen years before, and it was arranged by them, not as considering claims of priority, which have too often been occasion of unworthy wrangling, but in the " interests of science generally," that an abstract of Darwin's manuscript should be read with Wallace's paper at a meeting of the Linnæan Society on the 1st of July, 1858. The full title of the joint communication was On the Tendency of Species to form Varieties, and on the Perpetuation of Varieties and Species by Natural Selection. Sir Joseph Hooker, describing the gathering, says that " the interest excited was intense, but the subject was too novel and too ominous for the old school to enter the lists before armouring. After the meeting it was talked over with bated breath. Lyell's approval, and perhaps, in a small way mine, as his lieutenant in the affair, rather overawed the Fellows, who would otherwise have flown out against the doctrine. We had, too, the vantage ground of being familiar with

the authors and their theme." Nothing can deprive
Mr. Wallace of the honour due to him as the co-
originator of the theory, which, regarded in its application to the origin, history, and destiny of man, involves the most momentous changes in belief, and
there may be fitly quoted here his own modest and,
doubtless, correct, assessment of limitations which in
no wise invalidate his high claims. In the Preface
to his Contributions to the Theory of Natural Selection (1870), Mr. Wallace says the book will prove
that he both saw at the time the value and scope of
the law which he had discovered, and has since been
able to apply to some purpose in a few original lines
of investigation. " But," he adds, " here my claims
cease. I have felt all my life, and I still feel, the
most sincere satisfaction that Mr. Darwin had been
at work long before me, and that it was not left for
me to attempt to write the Origin of Species.   I
have long since measured my own strength, and
know full well that it would be quite unequal to
that task. Far abler men than myself may confess
that they have not that untiring patience in accumu-
lating, and that wonderful skill in using, large masses
of facts of the most varied kind—that wide and
accurate physiological knowledge—that acuteness in
devising and skill in carrying out experiments, and
that admirable style of composition at once clear,
persuasive, and judicial—qualities which, in their
harmonious combination, mark out Mr. Darwin as
the man, perhaps of all men now living, best fitted

for the great work he has undertaken and accomplished."

In a letter to Wallace dated 20th April, 1870, Darwin says, " There has never been passed on me, or, indeed, on any one, a higher eulogium than yours. I wish that I fully deserved it. Your modesty and candour are very far from new to me. I hope it is a satisfaction to you to reflect—and very few things in my life have been more satisfactory to me—that we have never felt any jealousy towards each other, though in one sense rivals. I believe I can say this of myself with truth, and I am absolutely sure it is true of you."

But on one question, and that round which discussion still rages, the friends were poles asunder. There had been correspondence between them as to the bearing of the theory of natural selection on man, and in April, 1869, Darwin wrote, " As you expected, I differ grievously from you, and I am very sorry for it. I can see no necessity for calling in an additional and proximate cause in regard to man." In the fifteenth chapter of his comprehensive book on Darwinism, Wallace admits the action of natural selection in man's physical structure. This structure classes him among the vertebrates; the mode of human suckling classes him among the mammals; his blood, his muscles, and his nerves, the structure of his heart with its veins and arteries, his lungs and his whole respiratory and circulatory systems, all closely correspond to those of other mammals, and are often almost identical with them. He possesses the same number of limbs, terminating in the same number of digits, as belong fundamentally to the mammals. His senses are identical with theirs, and his organs of sense are the same in number and occupy the same relative position. Every detail of structure which is common to the mammalia as a class is found also in man, while he differs from them only in such ways and degrees as the various species or groups of mammals differ from each other. He is, like them, begotten by sexual conjugation; like them, developed from a fertilized egg, and in his embryonic condition passes through stages recapitulating the variety of enormously remote ancestors of whom he is the perfected descendant. Full-grown, he appears as most nearly allied to the anthropoid or man-like apes; so much does his skeleton resemble theirs that, comparing him with the chimpanzee, we find, with very few exceptions, bone for bone, differing only in size, arrangement, and proportion.

Mr. Wallace, therefore, rejected the idea of man's special creation " as being entirely unsupported by facts, as well as in the highest degree improbable." *But he would not allow that natural selection explains the origin of man's spiritual and intellectual nature.* These, he argues, " must have had another origin, and for this origin we can only find an adequate cause in the unseen universe of Spirit." More detailed treatment of this argument will be given further on; here reference is made to it as furnishing the explanation why Mr. Wallace kept not his " first estate," and dropped out of the ranks of Pioneers of Evolution. Many subjects, as hinted above, have occupied his facile pen—land nationalization, causes of depression in trade, labourers' allotments, vaccination, *et hoc genus omne;* showing, at least, the prominence which all social matters occupy in the minds of the leading exponents of the theory of Evolution. For of this, as will be seen, both Herbert Spencer and Huxley supply cogent examples in their application of that theory to human interests. But it is as a defender, although on lines of his own not wholly orthodox, of supernaturalism, with attendant beliefs in miracles and the grosser forms of spiritualism, that Mr. Wallace appears in the character of opponent to the inclusion of man's psychical nature as a product of Evolution.

The arresting influence of these views when backed by honest, sincere, and eminent men of the type of Mr. Wallace, and when also supported by several prominent men of science, renders it desirable to show that modern psychism is but savage animism " writ large," and wholly explicable on the theory of continuity. In his book on Miracles and Modern Spiritualism, of which a revised edition, with chapters on Apparitions and Phantasms, was issued in 1895, Mr. Wallace contends that " Spiritualism, if true, furnishes such proofs of the existence of ethereal beings and of their power to act upon matter, as must revolutionise philosophy. It demonstrates the actuality of forms of matter and modes of being before inconceivable; it demonstrates mind without brain, and intelligence disconnected from what we know as the material body; and it thus cuts away all presumption against our continued existence after the physical body is disorganised and dissolved. Yet more, it demonstrates, as completely as the fact can be demonstrated, that the so-called dead are still alive; that our friends are still with us, though unseen, and guide and strengthen us when, owing to absence of proper conditions, they cannot make their presence known. It thus furnishes a *proof* of a future life which so many crave, and for want of which so many live and die in anxious doubt, so many in positive disbelief. It substitutes a definite, real, and practical conviction for a vague, theoretical, and unsatisfying faith. It furnishes actual knowledge on a matter of vital importance to all men, and as to which the wisest men and most advanced thinkers have held, and still hold, that no knowledge was attainable."

This claim, this tremendous claim, on behalf of the phenomena of spiritualism to supply an answer to " the question of questions; the ascertainment of man's relation to the universe of things; whence our race has come; to what goal we are tending," rests on the assumption with which Mr. Wallace starts, " Spiritualism, *if true.*"

The essay from which the above passages are quoted is preceded by references in detail to a considerable number of cases of "the appearance of preterhuman or spiritual beings," the evidence of which " is as good and definite as it is possible for any evidence of any fact to be." These ghost-stories, contrasted with the full-flavoured eerie tales of old, are feebly monotonous. The apparatus of the medium is limited: the phenomena are largely of the " horse-play " order. Through the whole series we vainly seek for some ennobling and exalting conception of a life beyond, some glimpses " behind the veil," only to find that the shades are but diluted or vulgarized parodies of ourselves; or that " the filthy are filthy still," like the departed bargee whose " communicating intelligence " (we quote from a recent book on spiritualism entitled The Great Secret) was as coarse-mouthed as when in the flesh. In considering, if it be deemed worth while, the evidence of genuineness of the occurrences, we are thrown, not on the honesty, but on the competency of the witnesses. The most eminent among these show themselves persons of undisciplined emotions. The distinguished physicist, Professor Oliver Lodge, who has been described to the writer by an intimate friend of the Professor as " longing to believe something,"argues that in dealing with psychical phenomena, a hazy, muzzy state of mind is better than a mind " keenly awake " and " on the spot " (see Address to the Society for Psychical Research, Proceedings, part xxvi, pp. 14, 15). With this may be compared a Mohammedan receipt for summoning spirits given in Klunzinger's Upper Egypt (p. 386): " Fast seven days in a lonely place, and take incense with you. Read a chapter 1001 times from the Koran. That is the secret, and you will see indescribable wonders; drums will be beaten beside you, and flags hoisted over your head, and you will see spirits." Thus have the dreamy Oriental Moslem and the self-hypnotized Western professor met together to elicit truth from trance.

Concerning the competence of Mr. Wallace himself to weigh, unbiassed, the evidence which comes before him, it suffices to cite the case of Eusapia Paladino, a Neapolitan " medium," who, in the words of one of her most ardent dupes, became " the unexpected instrument of driving conviction as to the reality of psychical manifestations by the invisible into the minds of many scientists." A number of distinguished savants testified to the genuineness of the woman's performances in Professor Richet's cottage on the Ile Roubant in the autumn of 1893. It was the serious and complete conviction of all of them (Lodge, Richet, Ochorowicz, and others) that " on no single occasion during the occurrence of an event recorded by them was a hand of Eusapia's free to execute any trick whatever." Mr. Maskelyne, such testimony notwithstanding, declared that the whole business was " the sorriest of trickeries," and, to the credit of the Society for Psychical Research, it undertook the expense of bringing Eusapia to England for the purpose of testing the genuineness of her doings. She was taken to a house in Cambridge, and detected as a vulgar impostor. Yet Mr. Wallace, in the new edition of his Miracles and Modern Spiritualism, describes all the phenomena occurring at Professor Richet's house as "not explicable as the result of any known physical causes," and, in a subsequent explanatory letter to the Daily Chronicle of 24th of January, 1896, expresses the opinion that "the Cambridge experiments, so far as they are recorded, only prove that Eusapia *might* have deceived, not that she actually and *consciously* did so." The integrity of Mr. Wallace is not to be doubted, but what becomes of his competence to judge when prejudice blinds itself to facts? Spiritualism, *if true*, demonstrates this and that about the unseen; but spiritualism, *proved to be untrue*, lacks half the dexterity of an astute conjurer, and the whole of his honesty. Every scientific man recognises the doctrine of the Conservation of Energy as a fundamental canon. But with those who regard the phenomena of Spiritualism as "not explicable" except by supernatural causes, it would seem that that doctrine, as also the not unimportant conditions of Time and Space, count for nothing. When we read their reports of the behaviour of mediums who project (of course, in the dark) "abnormal temporary prolongations" like pseudopodia, we should feel alike depressed and confounded were there not abundant proofs what wholly untrustworthy observers scientific specialists can be outside their own domain. As the writer has remarked elsewhere, minds of this type must be built in water-tight compartments. They show how, even in the higher culture, the force of a dominant idea may suspend or narcotize the reason and judgment, and contribute to the rise and spread of another of the epidemic delusions of which history supplies warning examples.

They also show that man's senses have been his arch-deceivers, and his preconceptions their abettors, throughout human history; that advance has been possible only as he has escaped through the discipline of the intellect from the illusive impressions about phenomena which the senses convey. Upon this matter the words of the late Dr. Carpenter may be quoted, words the more weighty because they are the utterance of a man whose philosophy was influenced by deep religious convictions: " With every disposition to accept facts when I could once clearly satisfy myself that they were facts, I have had to come to the conclusion that whenever I have been permitted to employ such tests as I should employ in any scientific investigation, there was either intentional deception on the part of interested persons, or else self-deception on the part of persons who were very sober-minded and rational upon all ordinary affairs of life." He adds further: " It has been my business lately to inquire into the mental condition of some of the individuals who have reported the most remarkable occurrences. I cannot—it would not be fair—say all I could with regard to that mental condition; but I can only say this, that it all fits in perfectly well with the result of my previous studies upon the subject, viz., that there is nothing too strange to be believed by those who have once surrendered their judgment to the extent of accepting as credible things which common sense tells us are entirely incredible."

The fact abides that the great mass of supernatural beliefs which have persisted from the lower culture till now, and which are still held by an overwhelming majority of civilized mankind, are referable to causes concomitant with man's mental development: causes operative throughout his history. The low intellectual environment of his barbaric past was constant for thousands of years, and his adaptation thereto .was complete. The intrusion of the scientific method in its application to man disturbed that equilibrium. But this, as yet, only superficially. Like the foraminifera that persist in the ocean depths, the great majority of mankind have remained, but slightly, if at all, modified; thus illustrating the truth of the doctrine of evolution in their psychical history. (For that doctrine does not imply all-round continuous advance. " Let us never forget," Mr. Spencer says in Social Statics, " that the law is—adaptation to circumstances, be they what they may.") Therefore the superstitions that still dominate the life of man, even in so-called civilized centres, are no stumbling-blocks to us. They are supports along the path of inquiry, because we account for their persistence. Thought and feeling have a common base, because man is a unit, not a duality. But the exercise of the one has been active from the beginnings of his history—indeed we know not at what point backward we can classify it as human or quasi-human—while the other, speaking comparatively, has but recently been called into play. So far as its influence on the modern world goes, may we not say that it began at least in the domain of scientific naturalism with the Ionian philosophers? Emotionally, we are hundreds of thousands of years old; rationally, we are embryos.

In other words, man wondered countless ages before he reasoned; because feeling travels along the line of least resistance, while thought, or the challenge by inquiry—therefore the assumption that there may be two sides to a question—must pursue a path obstructed by the dominance of custom, the force of imitation, and the strength of prejudice and fear. It is here that anthropology, notably that psychical branch of it comprehended under folk-lore, takes up the cue from the momentous doctrine of heredity; explains the persistence of the primitive; and the causes of man's tardy escape from the illusions of the senses, and the general conservatism of human nature. " Born into life! in vain, Opinions, those or these, unalter'd to retain the obstinate mind decrees," as in the striking illustration cited in

Heine's Travel-Pictures. " A few years ago Bullock dug up an ancient stone idol in Mexico, and the next day he found that it had been crowned during the night with flowers. And yet the Spaniard had exterminated the old Mexican religion with fire and sword, and for three centuries had been engaged in ploughing and harrowing their minds and implanting the seed of Christianity." The causes of error and delusion, and of the spiritual nightmares of olden time, being made clear, there is begotten a generous sympathy with that which empirical notions of human nature attributed to wilfulness or to man's fall from a high estate. Superstitions which are the outcome of ignorance can only awaken pity. Where the corrective of knowledge is absent, we see that it could not be otherwise. Where that corrective is present, but either perverted or not exercised, pity is supplanted by blame. In either case, we learn that the art of life largely consists in that control of the emotions and that diversion of them into wholesome channels, which the intellect, braced with the latest knowledge, can alone effect.

Therefore, discarding theories of revelation, spiritual illumination, and other assumed supra-mundane sources of knowledge, sufficing causes of abnormal mental phenomena are found in abnormal working of the mental apparatus. The investigation of hallucinations (Lat. *alucinor*, to wander in mind) leaves no doubt that they are the effect of a morbid condition of that intricate, delicately poised

11

structure, the nervous system, under which objects are seen and sensations felt when no corresponding impression has been made through the medium of the senses. When the nervous system is out of gear, voices, whether divine or of the dead, may be heard; and actual figures may be seen. A mental image becomes a visual image; an imagined pain a real pain, as the great physiologist, John Hunter, testified when he said, " I am confident that I can fix my attention to any part until I have a sensation in that part." Shakespere portrays the like condition when Macbeth attempts to clutch the dagger wherewith to stab Duncan:

> There's no such thing ;
> It is the bloody business which informs
> Thus to mine eyes.

This abnormal state, which sees things having no existence outside the " mind's eye," is no respecter of persons; the savage and the civilized are alike its victims. It may be organic or functional. Organic, when disease is present; functional, through excessive fatigue, lack of food or sleep, or derangement of the digestive system, causing the patient, as Hood says, " to think he's pious when he's only bilious." Under such conditions, hallucinations of all sorts possess the mind; hallucinations from which the true peptic, who, as Carlyle says, " has no system," is delivered. Only the mentally anæmic, the emotionally overwrought, the unbalanced, and the epileptic, are the victims, whether of the lofty illusions of august visions such as carried Saint Paul, Saint Theresa, and Joan of Arc, into the presence of the holiest; or hallucination of drowned cat, thin and " dripping with water," born of the disordered nerves of Mrs. Gordon Jones. To quote from Dr. Gower's Bowman Lecture (Nature, 4th July, 1895) on Subjective Visual Sensations, such as accompany fits, when, e. g., sensations of sight occur without the retina being stimulated:

The spectra perceived before epileptic fits vary widely. They may be stars or sparks, spherical luminous bodies, or mere flashes of light, white or coloured, still or in movement. Often they are more elaborate, distinct visions of faces, persons, objects, places. They may be combined with sensations from the other special senses, as with hearing and smell. In one case a warning, constant for years, began with thumping in the chest ascending to the head, where it became a beating sound. Then two lights appeared, advancing nearer with a pulsating motion. Suddenly these disappeared and were replaced by the figure of an old woman in a red cloak, always the same, who offered the patient something that had the smell of Tonquin beans, and then he lost consciousness. Such warnings may be called psychovisual sensations. The psychical element may be very strong, as in one woman whose fits were preceded by a sudden distinct vision of London in ruins, the river Thames emptied to receive the rubbish, and she the only survivor of the inhabitants.

Had a man of lesser renown and mental calibre than Mr. Wallace thrown the weight of his testimony into the scales in favour of spiritualism, there would have been neither necessity nor excuse for this digression. But both these pleas prevail when we find the co-formulator of the Darwinian theory among mediums and their dupes. The respectful attention which his words command: the tremendous claims which he makes on behalf of the phenomena at *séances* as proving the existence of soul apart from body after death, and as revealing the conditions under which it lives, have made incumbent the foregoing attempt to indicate what other explanation is given of those phenomena, showing how these fall in with all we know of man's tendencies to imperfect observation and self-deception, and with all that history tells of the persistence of animistic ideas.

A salutary lesson on the use and misuse of the imagination is thus taught. That which, under wholesome restraint, is the initiative and incentive of inquiry, of enterprise, and of noble ideas; unrestricted, leads the dreamer and the enthusiast into ingulfing quicksands of illusions and delusions. Hence the necessity of curbing a faculty so that in unison with reason, it works toward definite ends within the domain, marking man's limits of service. As Dr. Maudsley reminds us in his sane and sober book on Natural Causes and Supernatural Seeming, "not by standing out of Nature in the ecstasy of a rapt and over-strained idealism of any sort, but by large and close and faithful converse with Nature and human nature in all their moods, aspects, and relations, is the solid basis of fruitful ideas and the soundest mental development laid. The endeavour to stimulate and strain any mental function to an activity beyond the reach and need of a physical correlate in external nature, and to give it an independent value, is certainly an endeavour to go directly contrary to the sober and salutary method by which solid human development has taken place in the past, and is taking place in the present."

The story of Darwin's work must now be resumed. Shortly after the Linnæan meeting, he prepared a series of chapters which, always regarded by him as an " Abstract," ultimately took book form, and was published, under the title of the Origin of Species, on the 24th of November, 1859.

The story of the reception of the work is admirably told by Huxley in the chapter which he contributed to Darwin's Life and Letters, and it may be commended as useful reading to a generation which, drinking-in Darwinism from its birth, will not readily understand how such storm and outcry as rent the air, both in scientific as well as clerical quarters, could have been raised. "In fact," says Huxley, " the contrast between the present condition of public opinion upon the Darwinian question; between the estimation in which Darwin's views are now held in the scientific world; between the acquiescence, or, at least, quiescence, of the theologian of the self-respecting order at the present day, and the outburst of antagonism on all sides in 1858–59, when the new theory respecting the origin of species first became known to the older generation to which I belong, is so startling that, except for documentary evidence, I should be sometimes inclined to think my memories dreams." The like reflection arises when we consider the indifference with which books of the most daring and revolutionary character, both in theology and morals, are treated nowadays, in contrast to the uproar which greeted such a *brutum fulmen* as Essays and Reviews. As for Colenso's Pentateuch, and books of its type, orthodoxy has long taken them to its bosom.

So far as the larger number of naturalists, and of the intelligent public who followed their lead, were concerned, there was an absolutely open mind on the question of the mutation of species. There had been, as the foregoing sections of this book have shown, a long time of preparation and speculation. We certainly find the keynote of Evolution in Heraclitus, and more than two thousand years after his time Herbert Spencer, above all men, had removed it from the empirical stage, and placed it on a base broad as the facts which supported it. But it needed the leaven of the human and personal to stir it into life, and touch man in his various interests; and not all that Mr. Spencer had done in application of the theory of development to social questions and institutions could avail much till Darwin's theory gave it practical shape. Dissertations on the passage of the "homogeneous to the heterogeneous"; explanations of the theory of the evolution of complex sidereal systems out of diffused vapours of seemingly simple texture, interested people only in a vague and wondering fashion. But when Darwin illustrated the theory of the modification of life-forms by familiar examples gathered from his own experiments and observations, and from intercourse with breeders of pigeons, horses, and dogs, this went to men's "business and bosoms," and if the vulgar interpreted Darwinism, as some, who should know better, interpret it even now, as explaining man's descent from a monkey, or how a bear became a whale by taking to swimming, the thoughtful accepted it as a master-key unlocking not the mystery of origins or of causes of variations, but the mystery of the ceaselessly-acting agent which, operating on favourable variations, has brought about myriads of species from simple forms.

As Huxley reminds us in the passage quoted above, the attitude of the clergy toward the theory of Evolution has undergone an astounding change. Dr. Whewell remarked that every great discovery in science has had to pass through three stages. First, people said, " It is absurd " ; then they said, " It is contrary to the Bible " ; finally, they said, " We always knew that it was so." Thus it has been with Evolution. It is calmly discussed; even claimed as a " defender of the faith," at Church Congresses nowadays. It was not so in the sixties. Here and there a single voice was raised in qualified sympathy— Charles Kingsley showed more than this—but both in the Old and the New World the " drum ecclesias-

tic " was beaten.   Cardinal Manning declared Darwinism to be a " brutal philosophy, to wit, there is
no God and the ape is our Adam."   Protestant and
Catholic agreed in condemning it as " an attempt to
dethrone God " ; as " a huge imposture," as " tending to produce disbelief of the Bible," and " to do
away with all idea of God," as " turning the Creator
out of doors."   Such are fair samples to be culled
from the anthology of invective which was the staple
content of nearly every " criticism."   Occasionally
some parody of reasoning appears when the " argument " is advanced that there is " a simpler explanation of the presence of these strange forms among
the works of God in the fall of Adam," but even this
pseudo-concession to logic is rare; and one divine
had no hesitation in predicting the fate of Darwin
and his followers in the world to come.   " If," said a
Dr. Duffield in the Princeton Review, " the development theory of the origin of man shall, in a
little while, take the place—as doubtless it will—with
other exploded scientific speculations, then they who
accept it with its proper logical consequences will,
in the life to come, have their portion with those who
in this life ' know not God and obey not the Gospel
of His Son.' "   But the most notable attack came
from Samuel Wilberforce, then Bishop of Oxford, in
the Quarterly Review of July, 1860.   " It is," said
Huxley, in his review of Haeckel's Evolution of Man,
" a production which should be bound in good stout
calf, or better, asses' skin, by the curious book-col-

lector, together with Brougham's attack on the un-
dulatory theory of light when it was first propounded
by Young." The bishop declared " the principle of
natural selection to be absolutely incompatible with
the word of God" and as "contradicting the revealed relations of creation to its Creator." If by
"revealed relations" and the "word of God" the
Bible is intended, the evolutionist is in agreement
with the bishop. But, at this time of day, it seems
scarcely worth while to shake the dust off articles
which have gone the way of all purely controversial
matter, and justification for reference to them lies
only in the fact that the contest between the biologists and the bishops is not yet ended.

In contrast to all this, and in evidence of the
compromise by which theology is vainly striving to
justify itself, are these vague sentences from Archdeacon Wilson's address at the Church Congress at
Shrewsbury in the autumn of 1896: " It is scarcely
too much to say that the Theistic Evolutionist cannot
be otherwise than a practical Trinitarian, and cannot
find a difficulty in the Incarnation or in the doctrine
of the Holy Spirit." " Christian doctrine, apart from
the statement of historical facts, is the attempt to
create out of Christ's teachirg, a philosophy of life
which shall satisfy these needs (i. e., the needs of
humanity), and it will therefore remain the same in
substance. But the form in which that doctrine will
be presented must change with man's intellectual environment. The bearing of Evolution on Christian

doctrine is, therefore, in a word, to modify, not the doctrine, but the form in which it is expressed."

Postponing the story of the famous debate between Wilberforce and Huxley, the reception accorded to the Origin of Species by Darwin's scientific contemporaries may be noted. Herbert Spencer's position, as will be shown later on, was already distinctive: he was a Darwinian before Darwin. Hooker, Huxley,—who said that he was prepared to go to the stake, if needs be, in support of some parts of the book,—Bates, and Lubbock were immediate converts; so were Asa Gray and Lyell, but with reservations, for Lyell, whose creed was Unitarian, never wholly accepted the inclusion of man, " body soul, and spirit," as the outcome of natural selection. Henslow and Pictet went one mile, but refused to go twain; Agassiz, Murray, and Harvey would have none of the new heresy; neither would Adam Sedgwick, who wrote a long protest to Darwin, couched in loving terms, and ending with the hope that " we shall meet in heaven."   The attitude of Owen, if apparently neutral or tentative in open conversation, was, as an anonymous critic, deadly hostile.   Although it is not included in the list of his writings given in the Life by his grandson, he is known to have been the author of the critique on the Origin of Species in the Edinburgh Review of April, 1860.

At the outset of the article he speaks of Darwin's " seduction " of " several, perhaps the majority of our younger naturalists " by the homœopathic form of the transmutation of species presented to them under the phrase of natural selection. . . . " Owen has long stated his belief that some pre-ordained law or secondary cause is operative in bringing about the change . . . we therefore regard the painstaking and minute comparison by Cuvier of the osteological and every other character that could be tested in the mummified ibis, cat, or crocodile with those of species living in his time; and the equally philosophical investigation of the polyps operating at an interval of thirty thousand years in the building-up of coral reefs by the profound palæontologist of Neuchâtel (Agassiz is here referred to), as of far truer value in reference to the inductive determination of the question of the origin of species than the speculations of Demailler, Buffon, Lamarck, ' Vestiges,' Baden Powell, or Darwin " (p. 532).

Entangled in the meshes of this theory of a " pre-ordained law," which seems to bear some relation to Aristotle's " perfecting principle," and is in close alliance with the teaching of the great Cuvier, at whose feet Owen had sat, he remained to the end of his life a type of arrested development. While the Church cited him as an authority against the Darwinian theory, especially in its application to man's descent, there remained in the memory of his brother savants his lack of candour in never withdrawing the statement made by him, and demonstrated by Huxley as untrue, that the " hippocampus minor " in the human brain is absent from the brain of the ape.

As for the reception of the book abroad, the French savants were somewhat coy, but the Germans, with Haeckel at their head, were enthusiastic. Darwin had, like all prophets, more honour in other countries than in his own, Evolution being rechristened *Darwinismus.* Translation after translation of the Origin followed apace, and the personal interest that gathered round the central idea led to the perusal of the book by people who had never before opened a scientific treatise. Punch seized on it as subject of caricature; and writers of light verse found welcome material for " chaff " which the winds of oblivion have blown away, a stanza here and there surviving, as in Mr. Courthope's Aristophanic lines:

Eggs were laid as before, but each time more and more varieties
    struggled and bred,
Till one end of the scale dropped its ancestor's tail, and the other
    got rid of his head.
From the bill, in brief words, were developed the Birds, unless our
    tame pigeons and ducks lie ;
From the tail and hind legs, in the second-laid eggs, the apes,—
    and Professor Huxley !

Heeding neither squib, satire, nor sermon, Darwin, in the quiet of his Kentish home, went on rearranging old materials, collecting new materials, and verifying both, the outcome of this being his works on the Fertilization of Orchids and the Variation of Plants and Animals under Domestication, published in 1862 and 1867 respectively. Between these dates Huxley's Man's Place in Nature—logical supplement to the Origin of Species—appeared. But of this more anon.

Meanwhile, as already named, Mr. Patrick Matthew had in the Gardener's Chronicle of 7th April, 1860, drawn attention to an appendix to his book on Naval Timber and Arboriculture published in 1831, in which he anticipated Darwin and Wallace's theory as follows:

" The self-regulating adaptive disposition of organised life may, in part, be traced to the extreme fecundity of Nature, who, as before stated, has in all the varieties cf her offspring a prolific power much beyond (in many cases a thousandfold) what is necessary to fill up the vacancies caused by senile decay. As the field of existence is limited and pre-occupied, it is only the hardier, more robust, better-suited-to-circumstance individuals, who are able to struggle forward to maturity, these inhabiting only the situations to which they have superior adaptation and greater power of occupancy than any other kind; the weaker and less circumstance-suited being prematurely destroyed. This principle is in constant action; it regulates the colour, the figure, the capacities, and instincts; those individuals in each species whose colour and covering are best suited to concealment or protection from enemies, or defence from inclemencies or vicissitudes of climate, whose figure is best accommodated to health, strength, defence, and support; whose capacities and instincts can best regulate the physical energies to self-advantage according to circumstances—in such immense waste of primary and youthful life those only come to maturity from the strict ordeal by which Nature tests their adaptation to her standard of perfection and fitness to continue their kind by reproduction" (pp. 384, 385).

While speaking of difficulty in understanding some passages in Mr. Matthew's appendix, Darwin says that "the full force of the principle of natural selection" is there, and, in referring to it in a letter to Lyell, he adds that "one may be excused in not having discovered the fact in a work on Naval Timber!"

Five years after this, another pre-Darwinian was unearthed, and, like Patrick Matthew, in unsuspected company. Dr. W. C. Wells read a paper before the Royal Society in 1813 on a White Female Part of whose Skin resembles that of a Negro, but this was not published till 1818, when it formed part of a volume including the author's famous Two Essays upon Dew and Single Vision. In his Historical Sketch Darwin says that Wells "distinctly recognises the principle of natural selection, and this is the first recognition which has been indicated; but he applies it only to the races of man, and to certain characters alone. . . . Of the accidental varieties of man, which would occur among the first few and scattered inhabitants of the middle regions of Africa, some one would be better fitted than the others to bear the diseases of the country. This race would

consequently multiply, while the others would decrease; not only from their inability to sustain the
attacks of disease, but from their incapacity of con-
tending with their more vigorous neighbours."

When the simplicity of the long-hidden solution
is brought home, we can understand Huxley's reflection on mastering the central idea of the Origin:
" How extremely stupid not to have thought of
that!" Twelve years elapsed before Darwin followed
up his world-shaking book with the Descent of Man.
But the ground had been prepared for its reception
in the decade between 1860 and 1870. Quoting
Grant Allen's able summary of the advance of the
theory of Evolution in his Charles Darwin: " One
by one the few scientific men who still held out
were overborne by the weight of evidence. Geology
kept supplying fresh instances of transitional forms;
the progress of research in unexplored countries kept
adding to our knowledge of existing intermediate
species and varieties. During those ten years, Herbert Spencer published his First Principles, his
Biology, and the remodelled form of his Psychology;
Huxley brought out Man's Place in Nature, the
Lectures on Comparative Anatomy, and the Introduction to the Classification of Animals; Wallace
produced his Malay Archipelago and his Contributions to the Theory of Natural Selection (Bates, we
may here add to Mr. Allen's list, published his paper
on Mimicry in 1861, and his Naturalist on the
Amazons in 1863); and Galton wrote his admirable

work on Hereditary Genius, of which his own family
is so remarkable an instance. Tyndall and Lewes
had long since signified their warm adhesion. At
Oxford, Rolleston was bringing up a fresh generation of young biologists in the new faith; at Cambridge, Darwin's old university, a whole school of
brilliant and accurate physiologists was beginning to
make itself both felt and heard. In the domain of
anthropology, Tylor was welcoming the assistance of
the new ideas, while Lubbock was engaged on his
kindred investigations into the Origin of Civilization
and the Primitive Condition of Man. All these
diverse lines of thought both showed the widespread
influence of Darwin's first great work, and led up
to the preparation of his second, in which he dealt
with the history and development of the human race.
And what was thus true of England was equally
true of the civilized world, regarded as a whole:
everywhere the great evolutionary movement was
well in progress, everywhere the impulse sent forth
from the quiet Kentish home was permeating and
quickening the entire pulse of intelligent humanity."

The Origin of Species, as we have seen, was intended as a rough draft or preliminary outline of
the theory of natural selection. The materials which
Darwin had collected in support of that theory being
enormous, the several books which followed between
1859 and 1881, the year before his death, were expansions of hints and parts of the pioneer book.
The last to appear was that treating of The Forma-

tion of Vegetable Mould through the Action of Worms. It embodied the results of experiments which had been carried on for more than forty years, since, as far back as 1837, Darwin read a paper on the subject before the Geological Society. Reference to it recalls a story, characteristic of Darwin's innate modesty, told to the writer by the present John Murray. Darwin called on the elder Murray (presumably some time in 1880), and after fumbling in his coat-tail pocket, drew out a packet, which he handed to Murray with the timidity of an unfledged author submitting his first manuscript. " I have brought you," he said, " a little thing of mine on the action of worms on soil," and then paused as if in doubt whether Murray would care to run the risk of bringing out the book! One story leads to another, and our second relates to the burial of Darwin in Westminster Abbey. Among the signatures of members of Parliament, requesting Dean Bradley's consent to Darwin's interment there, was that of Mr. Richard B. Martin, partner in the well-known bank of that name, trading under the sign of the " Grasshopper." In his history of this old institution Mr. John B. Martin prints the following letter, which was received on the 27th of April, 1882, the day after Darwin's funeral:—

Sirs—We have this day drawn a check for the sum of £280, which closes our account with your firm. Our reasons for thus closing an account

12

opened so very many years ago are of so exceptional a kind that we are quite prepared to find that they are deemed wholly inadequate to the result. . . . They are entirely the presence of Mr. R. B. Martin at Westminster Abbey, not merely as giving sanction to the same as an individual, but appearing as one of the deputation from a Society which has especially become the indorser and sustainer of Mr. Darwin's theories.   —— & Co.

The accordance of a resting-place to Darwin's remains among England's illustrious dead in that Valhalla, was an irenicon from Theology to one whose theories, pushed to their logical issues, have done more than any other to undermine the supernatural assumptions on which it is built. Not that Darwin was a man of aggressive type. If he speaks on the high matters round which, like planet tethered to sun, the spirit of man revolves by irresistible attraction, it is with hesitating voice and with no deep emotion. A man of placid temper, in whom the observing faculties were stronger than the reflective, he was content to collect and co-ordinate facts, leaving to others the work of pointing out their significance, and adjusting them, as best they could, to this or that theory. It would be unjust to say of him what John Morley says of Voltaire, that " he had no ear for the finer vibrations of the spiritual voice," but we know from his own confessions, what limitations hemmed in his emotional nature. The

Life and Letters tells us that he was glad, after the
more serious work and correspondence of the day
were over, to listen to novels, for which he had a
great love so long as they ended happily, and contained " some person whom one can thoroughly love,
if a pretty woman, so much the better." But
strangely enough, he lost all pleasure in music, art,
and poetry after thirty. When at school he enjoyed
Thomson, Byron, and Scott; Shelley gave him intense delight, and he was fond of Shakespeare,
especially the historical plays; but in his old age
he found him " so intolerably dull that it nauseated
me."

This curious and lamentable loss of the higher æsthetic
tastes is all the odder, as books on history, biographies, and
travels (independently of any scientific facts which they may
contain), and essays on all sorts of subjects, interest me as
much as ever they did. My mind seems to have become a
kind of machine for grinding general laws out of large collections of facts, but why this should have caused the atrophy of
that part of the brain alone on which the higher tastes depend
I cannot conceive. A man with a mind more highly organised
or better constituted than mine would not, I suppose, have
thus suffered; and, if I had to live my life again, I would have
made a rule to read some poetry and listen to some music at
least once every week, for perhaps the parts of my brain now
atrophied would thus have been kept active through use. The
loss of these tastes is a loss of happiness, and may possibly be
injurious to the intellect, and more probably to the moral character, by enfeebling the emotional part of our nature.

It is often said that a man's religion concerns
himself only. So far as the value of the majority

of people's opinions on such high matters goes, this is true; but it is a shallow saying when applied to men whose words carry weight, or whose discoveries cause us to ask what is their bearing on the larger questions of human relations and destinies to which past ages have given answers that no longer satisfy us, or that are not compatible with the facts discovered. Whatever silence Darwin maintained in his books as to his religious opinions, intelligent readers would see that unaggressive as was the mode of presentments of his theory, it undermined current beliefs in special providence, with its special creations and contrivances, and therefore in the intermittent interference of a deity; thus excluding that supernatural action of which miracles are the decaying stock evidence.

Nor could they fail to ask whether the theory of natural selection by " descent with modification " was to apply to the human species. And when Darwin, already anticipated in this application by his more daring disciples, Professors Huxley and Haeckel, published his Descent of Man, with its outspoken chapter on the origin of conscience and the development of belief in spiritual beings, a belief subject to periodical revision as knowledge increased, it was obvious that the bottom was knocked out of all traditional dogmas of man's fall and redemption, of human sin and divine forgiveness. Therefore, what Darwin himself believed was a matter of moment. His answers to inquiries which were made public during his lifetime told us that while the varying circumstances and modes of life caused his judgment to often fluctuate, and that while he had never been an atheist in the sense of denying the existence of a God, " I think," he says, " that generally (and more and more as I grow older) but not always, an agnostic would be the most correct description of my state of mind." The chapter on Religion, although a part of the autobiography, is printed separately in the Life and Letters. As the following quotation shows, it is interesting as detailing a few of the steps by which Darwin reached that suspensive stage.

Whilst on board the Beagle I was quite orthodox, and I remember being heartily laughed at by several of the officers (though themselves orthodox) for quoting the Bible as an unanswerable authority on some point of morality. I suppose it was the novelty of the argument that amused them. But I had gradually come by this time—i. e., 1836 to 1839—to see that the Old Testament was no more to be trusted than the sacred books of the Hindoos. The question, then, continually rose before my mind, and would not be banished—is it credible that if God were now to make a revelation to the Hindoos he would permit it to be connected with the belief in Vishnu, Siva, etc., as Christianity is connected with the Old Testament? This appeared to me utterly incredible.

By further reflecting that the clearest evidence would be requisite to make any sane man believe in the miracles by which Christianity is supported—and that the more we know of the fixed laws of Nature the more incredible do miracles become—that the men at that time were ignorant and credulous to a degree almost incomprehensible by us, that the Gospels can not be proved to have been written simultaneously with the events, that they differ in many important details, far too important, as it seems to me, to be admitted as the usual inaccuracies of eye-witnesses : by such reflections as these, which I give not as having the least novelty or value, but as they influenced me, I gradually came to disbelieve in Christianity as a divine revelation. The fact that many false religions have spread over large portions of the earth like wildfire had some weight with me.

But I was very unwilling to give up my belief; I feel sure of this, for I can well remember often and often inventing daydreams of old letters between distinguished Romans, and manuscripts being discovered at Pompeii or elsewhere, which confirmed in the most striking manner all that was written in the Gospels. But I found it more and more difficult, with free scope given to my imagination, to invent evidence which would suffice to convince me. Thus disbelief crept over me at a very slow rate, but was at last complete. The rate was so slow that I felt no distress.

Although I did not think much about the existence of a personal God until a considerably later period of my life, I will here give the vague conclusions to which I have been driven. The old argument from design in Nature, as given by Paley, which formerly seemed to me so conclusive, fails, now that the law of natural selection has been discovered. We can no longer argue that, for instance, the beautiful hinge of a bivalve shell must have been made by an intelligent being, like the hinge of a door by a man. There seems to be no more design in the variability of organic beings, and in the action of natural selection, than in the course which the wind blows. But I have discussed this subject at the end of my book on the Variation of Domesticated Animals and Plants, and the argument there given has never, as far as I can see, been answered.

Without doubt, the influence of the conclusions deducible from the theory of Evolution are fatal to belief in the supernatural. When we say the super-

Photo by London Stereoscopic Co.

Herbert Spencer

natural, we mean that great body of assumptions out of which are constructed all theologies, the essential element in these being the intimate relation between spiritual beings, of whom certain qualities are predicated, and man. These beings have no longer any place in the effective belief of intelligent and unprejudiced men, because they are found to have no correspondence with the ascertained operations of Nature.

2. *Herbert Spencer.*

Contact with many " sorts and conditions of men " brings home the need of ceaselessly dinning into their ears the fact that *Darwin's theory deals only with the evolution of plants and animals from a common ancestry. It is not concerned with the origin of life itself, nor with those conditions preceding life which are covered by the general term,* Inorganic Evolution. Therefore, it forms but a very small part of the general theory of the origin of the earth and other bodies, " as the sand by the seashore innumerable," that fill the infinite spaces.

We have seen that speculation about the universe had its rise in Ionia. After centuries of discouragement, prohibition, and, sometimes, actual persecution, it was revived, to advance, without further serious arrest, some three hundred years ago. A survey of the history of philosophies of the origin of the cosmos from the time of the renascence of inquiry, shows that the great Immanuel Kant has not had his due. As remarked already, he appears to have been the first to put into shape what is known as the nebular theory. In his General Natural History and Theory of the Celestial Bodies; or an Attempt to Account for the Constitution and the Mechanical Origin of the Universe upon Newtonian Principles, published in 1775, he " pictures to himself the universe as once an infinite expansion of formless and diffused matter. At one point of this he supposes a single centre of attraction set up, and shows how this must result in the development of a prodigious central body, surrounded by systems of solar and planetary worlds in all stages of development. In vivid language he depicts the great world-maelstrom, widening the margins of its prodigious eddy, in the slow progress of millions of ages, gradually reclaiming more and more of the molecular waste, and converting chaos into cosmos. But what is gained at the margin is lost in the centre; the attractions of the central systems bring their constituents together, which then, by the heat evolved, are converted once more into molecular chaos. Thus the worlds that are lie between the ruins of the worlds that have been and the chaotic materials of the worlds that shall be; and in spite of all waste and destruction, Cosmos is extending his borders at the expense of Chaos."

Kant's speculations were confirmed by the celebrated mathematician, Laplace. He showed that the " rings " rotate in the same direction as the central body from which they were cast off; sun, planets, and moons (those of Uranus excepted) moving in a common direction, and almost in the same plane. The probability that these harmonious movements are the effects of like causes he calculated as 200,000 billions to one.

The observations of the famous astronomer, Sir William Herschel, which resulted in the discovery of binary or double stars, of star-clusters, and cloud-like nebulæ (as that term implies) were further confirmations of Kant's theory. And such modifications in this as have been made by subsequent advance in knowledge, notably by the doctrine of the Conservation of Energy (the hypothesis of Kant and Laplace being based on gravitation alone), affect not the general theory of the origin of the heavenly bodies from seemingly formless, unstable, and highly-diffused matter. The assumption of primitive unstableness and unlikeness squares with the unequal distribution of matter; with the movements of its masses in different directions, and at different rates; and with the ceaseless redistribution of matter and motion. For all changes of states are due to the rearrangement of the atoms of which matter is made up, resulting in the evolution of the seeming like into the actual unlike; of the simple into the more and more complex, till—speaking of the only planet of whose life-history we can have knowledge—with the cooling of the earth to a temperature permitting of the evolution of living matter, the highest complexity is reached in the infinitely diverse forms of plants and animals. Therefore, as our knowledge of matter is limited to the changes of which we assume it to be the vehicle, it would seem that science reduces the Universe to the intelligible concept of Motion.

Since the great discovery by Kirchoff, in 1859, of the meaning of the dark lines that cross the refracted sun-rays, the spectroscope has come as powerful evidence in support of the nebular theory, while the photographic plate is a scarcely less important witness. The one has demonstrated that many nebulæ, once thought to be star-clusters, are masses of glowing hydrogen and nitrogen gases; that, to quote the striking communication made by the highest authority on the subject, Dr. Huggins, in his Presidential Address to the British Association, 1891, "in the part of the heavens within our ken, the stars still in the early and middle stages of evolution exceed greatly in number those which appear to be in an advanced condition of condensation." The other, recording infallible vibrations on a sensitive plate, and securing accurate registration of the impressions, reveals, as in Dr. Roberts's grand photograph of the nebula in Andromeda, a central mass round which are distinct rings of luminous matter, these being separated from the main body by dark rifts or spaces. To quote Dr. Huggins once more, "We seem to have presented to us some stage of cosmical Evolution on a gigantic scale."

The great fact that lies at the back of all these

confirmations of the nebular theory is the fundamental identity of the stuff of which the universe is
made; a fact which entered into the prevision of the
Ionian cosmologists. Dr. Huggins says that " if the
whole earth were heated to the temperature of the
sun, its spectrum would resemble very closely the
solar spectrum."

In referring to this, there may be carrying of
" owls to Athens," but that re-statements may sometimes be needful has illustration in Lord Salisbury's
Presidential Address to the British Association, 1894,
wherein the assumed absence of oxygen and nitrogen
in the sun's spectrum is adduced as an argument
against the theory of the common origin of the
bodies of the solar system. Speaking of the predominant proportion of oxygen in the solid and
liquid substances of the earth, and of the pre-
dominance of nitrogen in our atmosphere, his lord-
ship asked, " if the earth be a detached bit whisked
off the mass of the sun, as cosmogonists love to tell
us, how comes it that, in leaving the sun, we cleaned
him out so completely of his nitrogen and oxygen
that not a trace of these gases remains behind to
be discovered even by the searching vision of the
spectroscope?" If Lord Salisbury had consulted
Dr. Huggins, or some foreign astronomer of equal
rank, as Dunér or Scheiner, he would not have put
a question exposing his ignorance, and unmasking
his prejudice. These authorities would have told
him that when a mixture of the incandescent vapours

of the metals and metalloids (or non-metallic elementary substances, to which class both oxygen and
nitrogen belong), or their compounds, is examined
with the spectroscope, the spectra of the metalloids
always yield before that of the metals. Hence the
absence of the lines of oxygen and other metalloids,
carbon and silicon excepted, among the vast crowd
of lines in the solar spectrum. Then, too, in extreme
states of rarefaction of the sun's absorbing layer,
the absorption of the oxygen is too small to be sensible to us.

"While the genesis of the Solar System, and of
countless other systems like it, is thus rendered com-
prehensible, the ultimate mystery continues as great
as ever. The problem of existence is not solved:
it is simply removed further back. The Nebular
Hypothesis throws no light on the origin of diffused
matter; and diffused matter as much needs account-
ing for as concrete matter. The genesis of an atom
is not easier to conceive than the genesis of a planet.
Nay, indeed, so far from making the universe a less
mystery than before, it makes it a greater mystery.
Creation by manufacture is a much lower thing than
creation by evolution. A man can put together a
machine; but he cannot make a machine develop
itself. The ingenious artisan, able as some have
been so far to imitate vitality as to produce a mechanical pianoforte player, may in some sort conceive how, by greater skill, a complete man might
be artificially produced; but he is unable to conceive

how such a complex organism gradually arises out of a minute structureless germ. That our harmonious universe once existed potentially as formless diffuse matter, and has slowly grown into its present organized state, is a far more astonishing fact than would have been its formation after the artificial method vulgarly supposed. Those who hold it legitimate to argue from phenomena to noumena, may rightly contend that the Nebular Hypothesis implies a First Cause as much transcending 'the mechanical God of Paley' as does the fetish of the savage."

This quotation is from an essay on the Nebular Hypothesis, which appeared in the Westminster Review of July, 1858, and which must, therefore, have been written before the eventful date of the reading of Darwin and Wallace's memorable paper before the Linnæan Society. The author of that essay is Mr. Herbert Spencer, and the foregoing extract from it may fitly preface a brief account of his life-work in co-ordinating the manifold branches of knowledge into a synthetic whole. In erecting a complete theory of Evolution on a purely scientific basis " his profound and vigorous writings," to quote Huxley, " embody the spirit of Descartes in the knowledge of our own day." Laying the foundation of his massive structure in early manhood, Mr. Spencer has had the rare satisfaction of placing the topmost stone on the building which his brain devised and his hand upreared. While the sheets of

this little book are being passed for press, there ar-
rives the third volume of the Principles of Sociology,
which completes Mr. Spencer's Synthetic Philosophy. In the preface to this, the venerable author
says:

"On looking back over the six-and-thirty years
which I have passed since the Synthetic Philosophy was commenced, I am surprised at my
audacity in undertaking it, and still more surprised
by its completion. In 1860 my small resources had
been nearly all frittered away in writing and publish-
ing books which did not repay their expenses; and
I was suffering under a chronic disorder, caused by
overtax of brain in 1855, which, wholly disabling
me for eighteen months, thereafter limited my work
to three hours a day, and usually to less. How insane my project must have seemed to onlookers,
may be judged from the fact that before the first
chapter of the first volume was finished, one of my
nervous breakdowns obliged me to desist.

"But imprudent courses do not always fail.
Sometimes a forlorn hope is justified by the event.
Though, along with other deterrents, many relapses,
now lasting for weeks, now for months, and once for
years, often made me despair of reaching the end,
yet at length the end is reached. Doubtless in
earlier years some exultation would have resulted;
but as age creeps on feelings weaken, and now my
chief pleasure is in my emancipation. Still there is
satisfaction in the consciousness that losses, dis-

couragements, and shattered health have not prevented me from fulfilling the purpose of my life."

These words recall a parallel invited by Gibbon's record of his feelings on the completion of his immortal work, when walking under the acacias of his garden at Lausanne, he pondered on the " recovery of his freedom, and perhaps the establishment of his fame," but with a " sober melancholy " at the thought that " he had taken an everlasting leave of an old and agreeable companion."

HERBERT SPENCER, spiritual descendant—*longo intervallo*—of Heraclitus and Lucretius, was born at Derby on the 27th of April, 1820. His father was a schoolmaster; a man of scientific tastes, and, it is interesting to note, secretary of the Derby Philosophical Association founded by Erasmus Darwin. In Mr. Spencer's book on Education there are hints of his inheritance of the father's bent as an observer and lover of Nature in the remark that, " whoever has not in youth collected plants and insects, knows not half the halo of interest which lanes and hedgerows can assume." He was articled in his seventeenth year to a railway engineer, and followed that profession until he was twenty-five. During this period he wrote various papers for the Civil Engineers' and Architects' Journal, and, what is of importance to note, a series of letters to the Nonconformist in 1842 on The Proper Sphere of Government (republished as a pamphlet in 1844), in which " the only point of community with the

general doctrine of Evolution is a belief in the modi-
fiability of human nature through adaptation to conditions, and a consequent belief in human pro-
gression." After giving up engineering, Mr. Spencer
joined the staff of the Economist, and while thus
employed, published, in 1850, his first important
book, Social Statics, or the Conditions essential to
Human Happiness specified, and the first of them
developed. In a footnote to the later editions of this
work Mr. Spencer points out a brace of para-
graphs in the chapter on General Considerations in
which " may be seen the first step toward the general doctrine of Evolution. After referring to the
analogy between the subdivision of labour, which
goes on in human society as it advances; and the
gradual diminution in the number of like parts and
the multiplication of unlike parts which are observable in the higher animals; Mr. Spencer says:

" Now, just the same coalescence of like parts and
separation of unlike ones—just the same increasing
subdivision of function—takes place in the development of society. The earliest social organisms consist almost wholly of repetitions of one element.
Every man is a warrior, hunter, fisherman, builder,
agriculturist, toolmaker. Each portion of the community performs the same duties with every other
portion; much as each slice of the polyp's body is
alike stomach, muscle, skin, and lungs. Even the
chiefs, in whom a tendency towards separateness of
function first appears, still retain their similarity to

the rest in economic respects. The next stage is distinguished by a segregation of these social units into a few distinct classes—warriors, priests, and slaves. A further advance is seen in the sundering of the labourers into different castes, having special occupations, as among the Hindoos. And, without further illustration, the reader will at once perceive, that from these inferior types of society up to our own complicated and more perfect one, the progress has ever been of the same nature. While he will also perceive that this coalescence of like parts, as seen in the concentration of particular manufactures in particular districts, and this separation of agents having separate functions, as seen in the more and more minute division of labour, are still going on.

"Thus do we find, not only that the analogy between a society and a living creature is borne out to a degree quite unsuspected by those who commonly draw it, but also that the same definition of life applies to both. This union of many men into one community—this increasing mutual dependence of units which were originally independent—this formation of a whole consisting of unlike parts—this growth of an organism, of which one portion cannot be injured without the rest feeling it—may all be generalized under the law of individuation. The development of society, as well as the development of man and the development of life generally, may be described as a tendency to individuate—*to become a thing*. And rightly interpreted, the mani-

13

fold forms of progress going on around us are uni-
formly significant of this tendency."

Homo sum: humani nihil a me alienum puto: " I
am a man and nothing human is foreign to me."
This oft-quoted saying of the old farmer in the Self-
Tormentor of Terence might be affixed as motto
to Herbert Spencer's writings from the tractate on
the Proper Sphere of Government to the concluding
volume of the Principles of Sociology. For thought
of human interests everywhere pervades them; social
and ethical questions are kept in the van throughout.
Philosophy is brought from her high seat to mix
in the sweet amenities of home, in the discipline of
camp, in the rivalry of market; and linked to conduct. Conduct is defined as " acts adjusted to ends,"
the perfecting of the adjustment being the highest
aim, so that " the greatest totality of life in self, in
offspring, and in fellow-men " is secured, the limit
of evolution of conduct not being reached, " until,
beyond avoidance of direct and indirect injuries to
others, there are spontaneous efforts to further the
welfare of others." Emerson puts this ideal into
crisp form when he speaks of the time in which a
man shall care more that he wrongs not his neighbour than that his neighbour wrongs him; then will
his " market-cart become a chariot of the sun."

That humanity is the pivot round which Mr.
Spencer's philosophic system revolves is seen in the
earliest Essays, and notably in his making mental
evolution the subject of the first instalment of his

Synthetic Philosophy. For, in the Principles of Psychology, published in 1855, he limits feeling or consciousness to animals possessing a nervous system, and traces its beginnings in the " blurred, undetermined feeling answering to a single pulsation or shock " (as for example, to go no lower down the life-scale, in the medusa or jelly-fish), to its highest form as self-consciousness, or knowing that we know, in man. This dominant element in Mr. Spencer's philosophy secures it a life and permanence which, had it been restricted to explaining the mechanics of the inorganic universe, it could never have possessed. It has been observed how the Darwinian theory aroused attention in all quarters because it touched human interests on every side. And, although less obvious to the multitude, the Synthetic Philosophy, dealing with all cosmic processes as purely mechanical problems, interprets " the phenomena of life (excluding the question of its origin), mind, and society, in terms of matter and motion." Anticipating the levelling of epithets against such apparent materializing of mental phenomena involved in that method, Spencer remarks on the dismay with which men, who have not risen above the vulgar conception which unites with matter the contemptuous epithets " gross " and " brute," regard the proposal to reduce the phenomena of Life, of Mind, and of Society, to a level which they think so degraded. " Whoever remembers that the forms of existence which the uncultivated speak of with so much scorn, are shown by the man of science to be the more marvellous in their attributes the more they are investigated, and are also proved to be in their ultimate natures absolutely incomprehensible—as absolutely incomprehensible as sensation, or the conscious something which perceives it—whoever clearly recognises this truth, will see that the course proposed does not imply a degradation of the so-called higher, but an elevation of the so-called lower. Perceiving, as he will, that the Materialist and Spiritualist controversy is a mere war of words,—in which the disputants are equally absurd, each thinking that he understands that which it is impossible for any man to understand,—he will perceive how utterly groundless is the fear referred to. Being fully convinced that no matter what nomenclature is used, the ultimate mystery must remain the same, he will be as ready to formulate all phenomena in terms of Matter, Motion, and Force, as in any other terms; and will rather indeed anticipate, that only in a doctrine which recognises the Unknown Cause as co-extensive with all orders of phenomena, can there be a consistent Religion, or a consistent Philosophy."

This is clear enough; yet such is the crass density of some objectors that eighteen years after the above was written, Mr. Spencer, in answering criticisms on First Principles, had to rebut the charge that he believed matter to consist of "space-occupying units, having shape and measurement."

The Principles of Psychology was both preceded
and followed by a series of essays in which the
process of change from the " homogeneous to the
heterogeneous," i. e., from the seeming like to the
actual unlike, was expounded. Mr. Spencer tells
us that in 1852 he first became acquainted with
Von Baer's Law of Development, or the changes
undergone in each living thing, from the general to
the special, during its advance from the embryonic
to the fully-formed state. That law confirmed the
prevision indicated in the passages quoted above
from Social Statics, and impressed him as one of
the three doctrines which are indispensable elements
of the general theory of Evolution. The other two
are the Correlation of the Physical Forces, or the
transformation of different modes of motion into
other modes of motion, as of heat or light into
electricity, and so forth, in Proteus-like fashion; and
the Conservation of Energy, or the indestructibility
of matter and motion, whatever changes or transformations these may undergo.

In permitting the quotation of the useful abstract
of the Synthetic Philosophy which, originally drawn
up for the late Professor Youmans, was imbodied
in a letter to the Athenæum of 22d of July, 1882, Mr.
Spencer was good enough to volunteer the following
details to the writer:—

" You are probably aware that the conception set
forth in that abstract was reached by slow steps during many years. These steps occurred as follows:—

1850. Social Statics: especially chapter General
      Considerations. (Higher human Evo-
      lution.)

1852. March. Development Hypothesis, in the
      Leader. (Evolution of species, *vid.*
      ante, p. 111.)

1852. April. Theory of Population, etc., in West-
      minster Review. (Higher human Evo-
      lution.)

1854. July. The Genesis of Science in British
      Quarterly Review. (Intellectual Evo-
      lution.)

1855. July. Principles of Psychology. (Mental
      Evolution in general.)

1857. April. Progress: its Law and Cause: West-
      minster Review. (Evolution at large.)

1857. April. Ultimate Laws of Physiology.
      National Review. (Another factor of
      Evolution at large.)

" From these last two Essays came the inception
of the Synthetic Philosophy. The first programme
of it was drawn up in January, 1858." . . .

When seeing Mr. Spencer on the subject of this
letter, he took the further trouble to point out certain
passages in the essays originally comprised in the
one volume edition of 1858 which contain germinal
ideas of his synthesis. That they are his selection
will add to the interest and value of their quotation,
revealing, as perchance they may, a fragment of the

autobiography which it is an open secret Mr. Spencer has written.

"That Law, Religion, and Manners are thus related—that their respective kinds of operation come under one generalisation—that they have in certain contrasted characteristics of men a common support and a common danger—will, however, be most clearly seen on discovering that they have a common origin. Little as from present appearances we should suppose it, we shall yet find that at first, the control of religion, the control of laws, and the control of manners, were all one control. However incredible it may now seem, we believe it to be demonstrable that the rules of etiquette, the provisions of the statute-book, and the commands of the decalogue, have grown from the same root. If we go far back enough into the ages of primeval Fetishism, it becomes manifest that originally Deity, Chief, and Master of the Cermonies were identical" (Essays, vol. i, 1883 edition; Manners and Fashion, p. 65).

"Scientific advance is as much from the special to the general as from the general to the special. Quite in harmony with this we find to be the admissions that the sciences are as branches of one trunk, and that they were at first cultivated simultaneously; and this becomes the more marked on finding, as we have done, not only that the sciences have a common root, but that science in general has a common root with language, classification, reasoning, art; that throughout civilisation these have advanced together, acting and reacting on each other just as the separate sciences have done; and that thus the development of intelligence in all its divisions and subdivisions has conformed to this same law to which we have shown the sciences conform" (Ib. The Genesis of Science, pp. 191, 192).

(In correspondence with this, recognising that the same method has to be adopted in all inquiry, whether we deal with the body or the mind, the following may be quoted from Hume's Treatise on Human Nature.

" 'Tis evident that all the sciences have a relation, greater or less, to human nature; and that, however wide any of them may seem to run from it, they still return back by one passage or another. Even *Mathematics, Natural Philosophy*, and *Natural Religion* are in some measure dependent on the science of MAN, since they lie under the cognisance of men, and are judged of by their powers and qualities.)

" The analogy between individual organisms and the social organisms is one that has in all ages forced itself on the attention of the observant. . . . While it is becoming clear that there are no such special parallelisms between the constituent parts of a man and those of a nation, as have been thought to exist, it is also becoming clear that the general principles of development and structure displayed in all organised bodies are displayed in societies also. The fundamental characteristic both of societies and of living creatures is, that they consist of mutually dependent parts; and it would seem that this involves a community of various other characteristics. . . . Meanwhile, if any such correspondence exists, it is clear that Biology and Sociology will more or less interpret each other.

" One of the positions we have endeavoured to establish is, that in animals the process of development is carried on, not by differentiations only, but by subordinate integrations. Now in the social organism we may see the same duality of process; and further, it is to be observed that the integrations are of the same three kinds. Thus we have integrations that arise from the simple growth of adjacent parts that perform like functions; as, for instance, the coalescence of Manchester with its calico-weaving suburbs. We have other integrations that arise when, out of several places producing a particular commodity, one monopolises more and more of the business, and leaves the rest to dwindle; as witness the growth of the Yorkshire cloth districts at the expense of those in the west of England. . . . And we have yet those other integrations that result from the actual approximation of the similarly-occupied parts, whence results such facts as the concentration of publishers in Paternoster Row, of lawyers in the Temple and neighbourhood, of corn merchants about Mark Lane, of civil engineers in Great George Street, of bankers in the centre of the city " (Essays, vol. iii, 1878 edition; Transcendental Physiology, pp. 414-416).

But, divested of technicalities, and summarized in words to be "understanded of the people," the following quotation from the Essay on Progress: Its Law and Cause, gives the gist of the Synthetic Philosophy:

"We believe we have shown beyond question that that which the German physiologists (Von Baer, Wolff, and others) have found to be the law of organic development (as of a seed into a tree, and of an egg into an animal), is the law of all development. The advance from the simple to the complex, through a process of successive differentiations (i. e., the appearance of differences in the parts of a seemingly like substance), is seen alike in the earliest changes of the Universe to which we can reason our way back; and in the earlier changes which we can inductively establish; it is seen in the geologic and climatic evolution of the Earth, and of every single organism on its surface; it is seen in the evolution of Humanity, whether contemplated in the civilised individual, or in the aggregation of races; it is seen in the evolution of Society in respect alike of its political, its religious, and its economical organisation; and it is seen in the evolution of all those endless concrete and abstract products of human activity which constitute the environment of our daily life. From the remotest past which Science can fathom, up to the novelties of yesterday, that in which Progress essentially consists, is the transformation of the homogeneous into the heterogeneous " (Essays, vol. i, 1883, p. 30).

To this may fitly follow the " succinct statement of the cardinal principles developed in the successive works," which Mr. Spencer, as named above, prepared for Professor Youmans.

1. Throughout the universe in general and in detail there is an unceasing redistribution of matter and motion.

2. This redistribution constitutes evolution when there is a predominant integration of matter and dissipation of motion, and constitutes dissolution when there is a predominant absorption of motion and disintegration of matter.

3. Evolution is simple when the process of integration, or the formation of a coherent aggregate, proceeds uncomplicated by other processes.

4. Evolution is compound, when along with this primary change from an incoherent to a coherent state, there go on secondary changes due to differences in the circumstances of the different parts of the aggregate.

5. These secondary changes constitute a transformation of the homogeneous into the heterogeneous—a transformation which, like the first, is exhibited in the universe as a whole and in all (or nearly all) its details; in the aggregate of stars and nebulæ; in the planetary system; in the earth as an inorganic mass; in each organism, vegetal or ani-

mal (Von Baer's law otherwise expressed); in the aggregate of organisms throughout geologic time; in the mind; in society; in all products of social activity.

6. The process of integration, acting locally as well as generally, combines with the process of differentiation to render this change not simply from homogeneity to heterogeneity, but from an indefinite homogeneity to a definite heterogeneity; and this trait of increasing definiteness, which accompanies the trait of increasing heterogeneity, is, like it, exhibited in the totality of things and in all its divisions and subdivisions down to the minutest.

7. Along with this redistribution of the matter composing any evolving aggregate there goes on a redistribution of the retained motion of its components in relation to one another; this also becomes, step by step, more definitely heterogeneous.

8. In the absence of a homogeneity that is infinite and absolute, that redistribution, of which evolution is one phase, is inevitable. The causes which necessitate it are these—

9. The instability of the homogeneous, which is consequent upon the different exposures of the different parts of any limited aggregate to incident forces.

The transformations hence resulting are—

10. The multiplication of effects. Every mass and part of a mass on which a force falls subdivides and differentiates that force, which thereupon pro-

ceeds to work a variety of changes; and each of these becomes the parent of similarly-multiplying changes; the multiplication of them becoming greater in proportion as the aggregate becomes more heterogeneous. And these two causes of increasing differentiations are furthered by

11. Segregation, which is a process tending ever to separate unlike units and to bring together like units—so serving continually to sharpen, or make definite, differentiations otherwise caused.

12. Equilibration is the final result of these transformations which an evolving aggregate undergoes. The changes go on until there is reached an equilibrium between the forces which all parts of the aggregate are exposed to and the forces these parts oppose to them.

Equilibration may pass through a transition stage of balanced motions (as in a planetary system) or of balanced functions (as in a living body) on the way to ultimate equilibrium; but the state of rest in inorganic bodies, or death in organic bodies, is the necessary limit of the changes constituting evolution.

13. Dissolution is the counter-change which sooner or later every evolved aggregate undergoes. Remaining exposed to surrounding forces that are unequilibrated, each aggregate is ever liable to be dissipated by the increase, gradual or sudden, of its contained motion; and its dissipation, quickly undergone by bodies lately animate, and slowly undergone by inanimate masses, remains to be undergone at an

indefinitely remote period by each planetary and stellar mass, which since an indefinitely distant period in the past has been slowly evolving; the cycle of its transformations being thus completed.

14. This rhythm of evolution and dissolution, completing itself during short periods in small aggregates, and in the vast aggregates distributed through space completing itself in periods immeasurable by human thought, is, so far as we can see, universal and eternal—each alternating phase of the process predominating now in this region of space and now in that, as local conditions determine.

15. All these phenomena, from their great features down to their minutest details, are necessary results of the persistence of force under its forms of matter and motion. Given these as distributed through space, and their quantities being unchangeable, either by increase or decrease, there inevitably result the continuous redistributions distinguishable as evolution and dissolution, as well as all these special traits above enumerated.

16. That which persists unchanging in quantity, but ever changing in form, under these sensible appearances which the universe presents to us, transcends human knowledge and conception—is an unknown and unknowable power, which we are obliged to recognise as without limit in space and without beginning or end in time.

All that is comprised in the dozen volumes which, exclusive of the minor works and the Sociological

Tables, form the great body of the Synthetic Philosophy, is the expansion of this abstract. The general lines laid down in that Philosophy have become a permanent way along which investigation will continue to travel. The revisions which may be called for will not affect it fundamentally, being limited to details, more especially in the settlement of the relative functions of individuals and communities, and cognate questions. Into these we cannot enter here. Suffice it, that to those who have the rare possession of sound mental peptics, no more nutritive diet can be recommended than is supplied by First Principles and the works in which its theses are developed. For those who, blessed with good digestion, lack leisure, there is provided in a convenient volume the excellent epitome which Mr. Howard Collins has prepared.

The prospectus of the then proposed issue of the series of works which, beginning with First Principles, ends with the Principles of Sociology (1862–1896), was issued by Mr. Spencer in March, 1860. Through his courtesy the writer has seen the documents which prove that the first draft of that prospectus was written out on the 6th of January, 1858, and that it was the occasion of an interesting correspondence between Mr. Spencer and his father—mainly in the form of questions from the latter—during that month. The record of these facts is of some moment as evidencing that the scheme of the Synthetic Philosophy took definite shape in 1857. Therefore, the Theory of Evolution, dealing with the universe *as a whole,* was formulated some months before the publication of the Darwin-Wallace paper, in which only *organic evolution* was discussed. The Origin of Species, as the outcome of that paper, showed that the action of natural selection is a sufficing cause for the production of new life-forms, and thus knocked the bottom out of the old belief in special creation.

The general doctrine of Evolution, however, is not so vitally related to that of natural selection that the two stand or fall together. The evidence as to the connection between the succession of past life-forms which, regard being had to the well-nigh obliterated record, has been supplied by the fossil-yielding rocks; and the evidence as to the unbroken development of the highest plants and animals from the lowest which more and more confirms the theory of Von Baer; alike furnish a body of testimony placing the doctrine of Organic Evolution on a foundation that can never be shaken. And, firm as that, stands the doctrine of Inorganic Evolution upon the support given by modern science to the speculations of Immanuel Kant.

There is the more need for laying stress on this because recent discussions, revealing divided opinions among biologists as to the sufficiency of natural selection as a cause of all modifications in the structure of living things, lead timid or half-informed minds to hope that the doctrine of Evolution may yet turn out not to be true. It is in such stratum of intelligence that there lurks the feeling, whenever some old inscription or monument verifying statements in the Bible is discovered, that the infallibility of that book has further proof. For example, until the present year, not a single confirmatory piece of evidence as to the story of the Exodus was forthcoming from Egypt itself. Even the inscription which has come to light does not, in the judgment of such an expert as Dr. Flinders Petrie, supply the exact confirmation desired. But let that irrefragable witness appear, and while the historian will welcome it as evidence of the sojourn of the Israelites in Egypt, thus throwing light on the movements of races, and adding to the historical value of the Pentateuch; the average orthodox believer will feel a vague sort of satisfaction that the foundations of his belief in the Trinity and the Incarnation are somehow strengthened.

3. *Thomas Henry Huxley.*

THOMAS HENRY HUXLEY was born at Ealing, on the 4th of May, 1825. Montaigne tells us that he was " borne between eleven of the clock and noone," and, with like quaint precision, Huxley gives the hour of his birth as " about eight o'clock in the morning." Speaking of his first Christian name, he humorously said that, by curious chance, his parents chose that of the particular apostle with whom, as the doubting member of the twelve, he had always felt most sympathy.

Concerning his father, who was " one of the mas-

14

ters in a large semi-public school" (the father of
Herbert Spencer, it will be remembered, was also a
schoolmaster), Huxley has little to say in the slight
autobiographical sketch reprinted as an introduction
to the first volume of the Collected Essays. On that
side, he tells us, he could find hardly any trace in
himself, except a certain faculty for drawing, and a
certain hotness of temper. "Physically and mentally," he was the son of his mother, "a slender
brunette, of an emotional and energetic tempera-
ment." His school training was brief and profitless;
his tastes were mechanical, and but for lack of means,
he would have started life in the same profession
which Herbert Spencer followed till he forsook
Messrs. Fox's office for journalism. So, with a certain shrinking from anatomical work, Huxley studied
medicine for a time under a relative, and in his seventeenth year entered the Charing Cross Hospital
School as a student. In those days there was no instruction in physics, and only in such branch of
chemistry as dealt with the nature of drugs. *Non
multa, sed multum,* and what was lacking in breadth
was, perhaps, gained in thoroughness. Huxley had
as excellent a teacher in Wharton Jones as the latter
had a promising pupil in Huxley, and in working
with the microscope, the evidence of that came in
his discovery of a certain root-sheath in the hair,
which has since then been known as "Huxley's
layer."

Up to the time of his studentship, he had been

left, intellectually, altogether to his own devices. He tells us that he was a voracious and omnivorous reader, " a dreamer and speculator of the first water, well endowed with that splendid courage in attacking any and every subject which is the blessed compensation of youth and inexperience." Among the books and essays that impressed him were Guizot's History of Civilization; and Sir William Hamilton's essay On the Philosophy of the Unconditioned which he accidentally came upon in an odd volume of the Edinburgh Review. This, he adds, was " devoured with avidity," and it stamped upon his mind the strong conviction " that on even the most solemn and important of questions, men are apt to take cunning phrases for answers; and that the limitation of our faculties, in a great number of cases, renders real answers to such questions, not merely actually impossible, but theoretically inconceivable." Thus, before he was out of his teens, the philosophy that ruled his life-teaching was taking definite shape.

In 1845, he won his M. B. London with honours in anatomy and physiology, and after a few months' practice at the East End, applied, at the instance of his senior fellow-student, Mr. (afterwards Sir) Joseph Fayrer, for an appointment in the medical service of the Navy. At the end of two months he was fortunate enough to be entered on the books of Nelson's old ship, the Victory, for duty at Haslar Hospital. His official chief was the famous Arctic Explorer, Sir John Richardson, through whose recommendation he was appointed, seven months later, assistant surgeon of the Rattlesnake. That ship, commanded by Captain Owen Stanley, was commissioned to survey the intricate passage within the Barrier Reef skirting the eastern shores of Australia, and to explore the sea lying between the northern end of that reef and New Guinea. It was the best apprenticeship to what was eventually the work of Huxley's life—the solution of biological problems and the indication of their far-reaching significance. Darwin and Hooker had passed through a like marine curriculum. The former served as naturalist on board the Beagle when she sailed on her voyage round the world in 1831; the latter as assistant-surgeon on board the Erebus on her Antarctic Expedition in 1839. Fortune was to bring the three shoulder to shoulder when the battle against the theory of the immutability of species was fought.

During his four-years' absence Huxley, in whom the biologist dominated the doctor, made observations on the various marine animals collected. These he sent home to the Linnæan Society in vain hope of acceptance. A more elaborate paper to the Royal Society, communicated through the Bishop of Norwich (author of a book on birds, and father of Dean Stanley), secured the coveted honour of publication, and on Huxley's return in 1850 a " huge packet of separate copies" awaited him. It dealt with the anatomy and affinities of the Medusæ, and the original research which it evidenced justified his election in 1851 to the fellowship of the society whose presidential chair he was in after years to adorn. He would seem to have won the blue ribbon of science *per saltum*. Probably, so far as their biological value is concerned, nothing that he did subsequently has surpassed his contributions to scientific literature at that period; but if his services to knowledge had been limited to the class of work which they represent, he would have remained only a distinguished specialist. Further recognition of his well-won position came in the award of the society's royal medal. But fellowships and medals keep no wolf from the door, and Huxley was a poor man. After vain attempts to obtain, first, a professorship of physiology in England, and then a chair of natural history at Toronto (Tyndall was at the same time an unsuccessful candidate for the chair of physics in the same university), a settled position was secured by Sir Henry de la Beche's offer of the professorship of palæontology and of the lectureship on natural history in the Royal School of Mines, vacated by Edward Forbes. That was in 1854. Between that date and the time of his return Huxley had contributed a number of valuable papers on the structure of the invertebrates, and on histology, or the science of tissues. But these, while adding to his established qualifications for a scientific appointment, demand no detailed reference here. With both chairs there was united the curatorship of the fossil collections in the Museum of Practical Geology, and these, with

the inspectorship of salmon fisheries, which office he
accepted in 1881, complete the list of Huxley's more
important public appointments. He surrendered
them all in 1885, having reached the age at which,
as he jocosely remarked to the writer, " Every scientific man ought to be poleaxed." Perhaps he
dreaded the conservatism of attitude, the non-recep-
tivity to new ideas, which often accompany old age.
But for himself such fears were needless. He was
never of robust constitution; in addition to the lasting effects of an illness in boyhood, Carlyle's " accursed Hag," dyspepsia, which troubled both Darwin and Bates for the rest of their lives after their
return from abroad, troubled him. Therefore, considerations of health mainly prompted the surrender
of his varied official responsibilities, the loyal discharge of which met with becoming recognition in
the grant of a pension. This secured a modest competence in the evening of life to one who had never
been wealthy, and who had never coveted wealth.
To Huxley may fitly be applied what Faraday said
of himself, that he had " no time to make money."
And yet, to his abiding discredit, the present editor
of Punch allowed his theological animus, which had
already been shown in abortive attempts in the pages
of that " facetious " journal to appraise a Roman
Catholic biologist at the expense of Huxley, to further degrade itself by affixing the letters " L. S. D."
to his name in a character-sketch.

His public life may be said to date from 1854.

The duties which he then undertook included the delivery of a course of lectures to working men every alternate year. Some of these—models of their kind—have been reissued in the Collected Essays. Among the most notable are those on Our Knowledge of the Causes of the Phenomena of Organic Nature. At the outset of his public career lecturing was as distasteful to him as in earlier years the trouble of writing was detestable. But mother wit and "needs must" trained him in a short time to win the ear of an audience. One evening in 1852 he made his début at the Royal Institution, and the next day he received a letter charging him with every possible fault that a lecturer could commit— ungraceful stoop, awkwardness in use of hands, mumbling of words, or dropping them down the shirt front. The lesson was timely, and its effect salutary. Huxley was fond of telling this story, and it is worth recording—if but as encouragement to stammerers who have something to say—at what price he "bought this freedom" which held an audience spellbound. How he thus held it in later years they will remember who in the packed theatre of the Royal Institution listened on the evening of Friday, 9th of April, 1880, to his lecture On the Coming of Age of the Origin of Species.

In 1856 Huxley visited the glaciers of the Alps with Tyndall, the result appearing in their joint authorship of a paper on Glacial Phenomena in the Philosophical Transactions of the following year.

But this was a rare interlude. What time could be wrested from daily routine was given to the study of invertebrate and vertebrate morphology, palæon- tology, and ethnology, familiarity with which was no mean equipment for the conflict soon to rage round these seemingly pacific materials when their deep import was declared. The outcome of such varied industry is apparent to the student of scientific me- moirs. But a recital of the titles of papers con- tributed to these, as e. g., On Ceratodus, Hypero- dapedon Gordoni, Hypsilophodon, Telerpeton, and so forth, will not here tend to edification. The original and elaborate investigations which they em- body have had recognition in the degrees and medals which decorated the illustrious author. But it is not by these that Huxley's renown as one of the most richly-endowed and widely-cultured personalities of the Victorian era will endure. They might sink into the oblivion which buries most purely technical work without in any way affecting that foremost place which he fills in the ranks of philosophical biolo- gists both as clear-headed thinker and luminous in- terpreter.

In this high function the publication of the Ori- gin of Species gave him his opportunity. That was in 1859. As with Hooker and Bates, his experiences as a traveller, and, more than this, his penetrating inquiry into significances and relations, prepared his mind for acceptance of the theory of descent with modification of living forms from one stock. Hence the mutability, as against the old theory of the fixity, of species.

In the chapter On the Reception of the Origin of Species, which Huxley contributed to Darwin's Life and Letters, he gives an interesting account of his attitude toward that burning question. He says—

"I think that I must have read the Vestiges (see p. 119) before I left England in 1846, but if I did the book made very little impression upon me, and I was not brought into serious contact with the 'species' question until after 1850. At that time I had long done with the Pentateuchal cosmogony which had been impressed upon my childish under-standing as Divine truth with all the authority of parents and instructors, and from which it had cost me many a struggle to get free. But my mind was unbiassed in respect of any doctrine which presented itself if it professed to be based on purely philo-sophical and scientific reasoning. . . . I had not then and I have not now the smallest *a priori* objection to raise to the account of the creation of animals and plants given in Paradise Lost, in which Milton so vividly embodies the natural sense of Genesis. Far be it from me to say that it is untrue because it is impossible. I confine myself to what must be regarded as a modest and reasonable request for some particle of evidence that the existing species of animals and plants did originate in that way as a condition of my belief in a statement which appears to me to be highly improbable. . . .

"And by way of being perfectly fair, I had exactly the same answer to give to the evolutionists of 1851–58. Within the ranks of the biologists of that time I met with nobody, except Dr. Grant, of University College, who had a word to say for Evolution, and his advocacy was not calculated to advance the cause. Outside these ranks the only person known to me whose knowledge and capacity compelled respect, and who was at the same time a thoroughgoing evolutionist, was Mr. Herbert Spencer, whose acquaintance I made, I think, in 1852, and then entered into the bonds of a friendship which I am happy to think has known no interruption. Many and prolonged were the battles we fought on this topic. But even my friend's rare dialectic skill and copiousness of apt illustration could not drive me from my agnostic position. I took my stand upon two grounds: firstly, that up to that time the evidence in favour of transmutation was wholly insufficient; and secondly, that no suggestion respecting the causes of the transmutation assumed which had been made was in any way adequate to explain the phenomena. Looking back at the state of knowledge at that time, I really do not see that any other conclusion was justifiable.

"As I have already said, I imagine that most of those of my contemporaries who thought seriously about the matter were very much in my own state

of mind—inclined to say to both Mosaists and Evolutionists 'A plague on both your houses!' and
disposed to turn aside from an interminable and apparently fruitless discussion to labour in the fertile
fields of ascertainable fact. And I may therefore
further suppose that the publication of the Darwin
and Wallace papers in 1858, and still more that of
the Origin in 1859, had the effect upon them of the
flash of light, which to a man who has lost himself in a dark night suddenly reveals a road which,
whether it takes him straight home or not, certainly
goes his way. That which we were looking for and
could not find was a hypothesis respecting the origin
of known organic forms which assumed the operation of no causes but such as could be proved to be
actually at work. We wanted, not to pin our faith
to that or any other speculation, but to get hold of
clear and definite conceptions which could be
brought face to face with facts, and have their
validity tested. The Origin provided us with the
working hypothesis we sought. Moreover, it did the
immense service of freeing us for ever from the dilemma—refuse to accept the creation hypothesis,
and what have you to propose that can be accepted
by any cautious reasoner? In 1857 I had no answer
ready, and I do not think that any one else had.
A year later we reproached ourselves with dulness for
being perplexed by such an inquiry. My reflection,
when I first made myself master of the central idea
of the Origin was 'How extremely stupid not to

have thought of that!' I suppose that Columbus's companions said much the same when he made the egg stand on end. The facts of variability, of the struggle for existence, of adaptation to conditions, were notorious enough, but none of us had suspected that the road to the heart of the species problem lay through them, until Darwin and Wallace dispelled the darkness, and the beacon-fire of the Origin guided the benighted."

But the disciple soon outstripped the master. As was said of Luther in relation to Erasmus, Huxley hatched the egg that Darwin laid. For in the Origin of Species the theory was not pushed to its obvious conclusion: Darwin only hinted that it " would throw much light on the origin of man and his history." His silence, as he candidly tells us in the Introduction to the Descent of Man, was due to a desire " not to add to the prejudices against his views." No such hesitancy kept Huxley silent. In the spirit of Plato's Laws, he followed the argument whithersoever it led. In 1860 he delivered a course of lectures to working-men On the Relaticns of Man to the Lower Animals, and in 1862, a couple of lectures on the same subject at the Edinburgh Philosophical Institution. The important and significant feature of these discourses was the demonstration that no cerebral barrier divides man from apes; that the attempt to draw a psychical distinction between him and the lower animals is futile; and that " even the highest faculties of feeling and of intellect begin to germinate in lower forms of life." The lectures were published in 1863 in a volume entitled Evidence as to Man's Place in Nature; and it was with pride warranted by the results of subsequent researches that Huxley, in a letter to the writer, thus refers to the book when arranging for its reissue among the Collected Essays—

I was looking through Man's Place in Nature the other day. I do not think there is a word I need delete, nor anything I need add, except in confirmation and extension of the doctrine there laid down. That is great good fortune for a book thirty years old, and one that a very shrewd friend of mine implored me not to publish, as it would certainly ruin all my prospects.

The sparse annotations to the whole series of reprinted matter show that the like permanence attends all his writings. And yet, true workman, with ideal ever lying ahead, as he was, he remarked to the writer that never did a book come hot from the press, but he wished that he could suppress it and rewrite it.

But before dealing with the momentous issues raised in Man's Place in Nature, we must return to 1860. For that was the " Sturm und Drang " period. Then, at Oxford, " home of lost causes," as Matthew Arnold apostrophizes her in the Preface to his Essays in Criticism, was fought, on Saturday, 30th of June, a memorable duel between biologist and bishop; perhaps in its issues, more memorable than the historic discussion on the traditional doctrine of special creation between Cuvier and Geoffroy Saint-Hilaire in the French Academy in 1830.

Both Huxley and Wilberforce were doughty champions. The scene of combat, the Museum Library, was crammed to suffocation. Fainting women were carried out. There had been " words " between Owen and Huxley on the previous Thursday. Owen contended that there were certain fundamental differences between the brains of man and apes. Huxley met this with " direct and unqualified contradiction," and pledged himself to " justify that unusual procedure elsewhere." No wonder that the atmosphere was electric. The bishop was up to time. Declamation usurped the vacant place of argument in his speech, and the declamation became acrid. He finished his harangue by asking Huxley whether he was related by his grandfather's or grandmother's side to an ape. " The Lord hath delivered him into my hands," whispered Huxley to a friend at his side, as he rose to reply. After setting his opponent an example in demonstrating his case by evidence which, although refuting Owen, evoked no admission of error from him then or ever after, Huxley referred to the personal remark of Wilberforce. And this is what he said—

I asserted, and I repeat, that a man has no reason to be ashamed of having an ape for his grandfather. If there were an ancestor whom I should feel shame in recalling, it would be a *man*, a man of restless and versatile intellect, who, not content with an equivocal success in his own sphere of activity, plunges into scientific questions with which he has no real acquaintance, only to obscure them by an aimless rhetoric, and distract the attention of his hearers from the real point at issue by eloquent digressions, and skilled appeals to religious prejudice.

Perhaps the best comment on a piece of what is now ancient history is to quote the admissions made by Lord Salisbury—a rigid High Churchman—in his presidential address to the British Association in this same city of Oxford in 1894—

Few now are found to doubt that animals separated by differences far exceeding those that distinguish what we know as species have yet descended from common ancestors. . . . Darwin has, as a matter of fact, disposed of the doctrine of the immutability of species.

Few, also, are now found to doubt not only that doctrine, but also the doctrine that all life-forms have a common origin; plants and animals being alike built-up of matter which is identical in character. This doctrine, to-day a commonplace of biology, was, thirty years ago, rank heresy, since it seemed to reduce the soul of man to the level of his biliary duct. Hence the Oxford storm was but a capful of wind compared with that which raged round Huxley's lecture on The Physical Basis of Life delivered, thus aggravating the offence, on a " Sabbath " evening in Edinburgh in 1868. People had settled down, with more or less vague understanding of the matter, into quiescent acceptance of Darwinism. And now their somnolence was rudely shaken by this Southron troubler of Israel, with his production of a bottle of solution of smelling salts, and a pinch or two of other ingredients, which represented the elementary substances entering into the composition of every living thing from a jelly-speck to man. Well might the removal of the stopper to that bottle take their breath away! Microscopists, philosophers " so-called," and clerics alike raised the cry of " gross materialism," never pausing to read Huxley's anticipatory answer to the baseless charge, an answer repeated again and again in his writings, as in the essay on Descartes's Discourse touching the method of using one's reason rightly, and in his Hume. In season and out of season he never wearies in insisting that there is nothing in the doctrine inconsistent with the purest idealism. " All the phenomena of Nature are, in their ultimate analysis, known to us only as facts of consciousness." The cyclone thus raised travelled westward on the heels of Tyndall, when in 1874 he asserted the fundamental identity of the organic and inorganic; dashing, as his Celtic blood stirred him, the statements with a touch of poetry in the famous phrase that " the genius of Newton was potential in the fires of the sun."

The ancient belief in " spontaneous generation," which Redi's experiments upset, was the subject of Huxley's Presidential Address to the British Association in 1870. But while he showed how subsequent investigation confirmed the doctrine of Abiogenesis, or the non-production of living from dead matter, he made this statement in support of Tyndall's creed as to the fundamental unity of the vital and the non-vital.

" Looking back through. the prodigious vista of the past, I find no record of the commencement of life, and therefore I am devoid of any means of forming a definite conclusion as to the conditions of its appearance. Belief, in the scientific sense of the word, is a serious matter, and needs strong foundations. To say, therefore, in the admitted absence of evidence, that I have any belief as to the mode in which the existing forms of life have originated, would be using words in a wrong sense. But expectation is permissible where belief is not; and if it were given to me to look beyond the abyss of geologically recorded time to the still more remote period when the earth was passing through physical and chemical conditions which it can no more see again than a man can recall his infancy, I should expect to be a witness of the evolution of living protoplasm from non-living matter. I should expect to see it appear under forms of great simplicity, endowed, like existing fungi, with the power of determining the formation of new protoplasm from such matters as ammonium carbonates, oxalates, and tartrates, alkaline and earthy phosphates, and water, without the aid of light. That is the expectation to which analogical reasoning leads me; but I beg you once more to recollect that I have no right to call my opinion anything but an act of philosophical faith."

15

Huxley was the Apostle Paul of the Darwinian movement, and one main result of his active propagandism was to so effectively prepare the way for the reception of the profounder issues involved in the theory of the origin of species, that the publication of Darwin's Descent of Man in 1871 created mild excitement. And the weight of his support is the greater because he never omitted to lay stress on the obscurity which still hides the causes of variation which, it must be kept in mind, natural selection cannot bring about, and on which it can only act. He insists on the non-implication of the larger theory with its subordinate parts, or with the fate of them. The "doctrine of Evolution is a generalisation of certain facts which may be observed by any one who will take the necessary trouble." The facts are those which biologists class under the heads of Embryology and Palæontology, to the conclusions from which "all future philosophical and theological speculations will have to accommodate themselves."

That is the direction of the revolution to which the publication of Man's Place in Nature gave impetus; and it is in the all-round application of the theory of man's descent that Huxley stands foremost, both as leader and lawgiver. Mr. Spencer has never shrunk from controversy, but he has not forsaken the study for the arena, and hence his influence, great and abiding as it is, has been less direct and personal than that of his comrade, "ever a fighter," who, in Browning's words, "marched breast

forward." Man's Place in Nature was the first of a
series of deliverances upon the most serious questions that can occupy the mind; and its successors,
the brilliant monograph on Hume, published in
1879, and the Romanes Lecture on Evolution and
Ethics, delivered at Oxford, 18th of May, 1893, are
but expansions of the thesis laid down in that wonderful little volume; wonderful in the prevision which
fills it, and in the justification which it has received
from all subsequent research, notably in psychology.

If the propositions therein maintained are un-
shaken, then there is no possible reconciliation between Evolution and Theology, and all the smooth
sayings in attempted harmonies between the two,
of which Professor Drummond's Ascent of Man is a
type, and in speeches at Church Congresses of which
that delivered by Archdeacon Wilson (see p. 161) is
a type, do but hypnotize the "light half-believers of
our casual creeds." To some there are "signs of the
times" which point to approaching acquiescence in
the sentiment of Ovid, paralleled by a famous passage in Gibbon, that "the existence of the gods is a
matter of public policy, and we must believe it accordingly." It looks like the prelude to surrender
of what is the cardinal dogma of Christianity when
we read in the Archdeacon's address that "the theory of Evolution is indeed fatal to certain *quasi-*
mythological doctrines of the Atonement which once
prevailed, but it is in harmony with its spirit." For
those doctrines, as the Venerable apologist may learn

from the evidence in Frazer's Golden Bough (chap. iii, *passim*), are wholly mythological, because barbaric. But, in truth, there is not a dogma of Christendom, not a foundation on which the dogma rests, that Evolution does not traverse. The Church of England adopts " as thoroughly to be received and believed," the three ancient creeds, known as the Apostles', the Athanasian, and the Nicene. There is not a sentence in any one of these which finds confirmation; and only a sentence or two that find neither confirmation nor contradiction, in Evolution.

The question, on which reams of paper have been wasted, lies in a nutshell. The statements in the Creeds profess to have warrant in the direct words of the Bible; or in inferences drawn from those words, as defined by the Councils of the Church. The decisions of these Councils represent the opinion of the majority of fallible men composing those assemblies, and no number of fallible parts can make an infallible whole. As Selden quaintly puts it (Table Talk, xxx, Councils), " they talk (but blasphemously enough) that the Holy Ghost is president of their General Councils, when the truth is the odd man is still the Holy Ghost." With this same " odd man " rested the decision as to what books should be included or excluded from the collection on which the Church bases its authority and formulates its creeds. So, in the last result, both sets of questions are settled by a human tribunal employing a circular argument. But, dismissing this for the moment, let us see to what issues the controversy is narrowed, to quote Huxley's words (written in 1871), by "the spontaneous retreat of the enemy from nine-tenths of the territory which he occupied ten years ago."

The battle has no longer to be fought over the question of the fundamental identity of the physical structure of man and of the anthropoid apes. The most enlightened Protestant divines accept this as proven; and not a few Catholic divines are adopting an attitude toward it which is only the prelude to surrender. Matters must have moved apace in the Church which Huxley, backed by history, describes as "that vigorous and consistent enemy of the highest intellectual, moral, and social life of mankind," to permit the Roman Catholic Professor of Physics in the University of Notre Dame, America, to parley as follows:

"Granting that future researches in palæontology, anthropology, and biology, shall demonstrate beyond doubt that man is genetically related to the inferior animals, and we have seen how far scientists are from such a demonstration (?), there will not be, even in such an improbable event, the slightest ground for imagining that then, at last, the conclusions of science are hopelessly at variance with the declarations of the sacred text, or the authorised teachings of the Church of Christ. All that would logically follow from the demonstration of the animal origin of man, would be a modification of the traditional view regarding the origin of the body of our first ancestor. We should be obliged to revise the interpretation that has usually been given to the words of Scripture which refer to the formation of Adam's body, and read these words in the sense which Evolution demands, a sense which, as we have seen, may be attributed to the words of the inspired record, without either distorting the meaning of terms, or in any way doing violence to the text" (Evolution and Dogma. By the Reverend J. A. Zahm, Ph. D., C. S. C., pp. 364, 365).

Upon this suggested revision of writings which are claimed as forming part of a divine revelation, one of the highest authorities, Francisco Suarez, thus refers, in his Tractatus de Opere sex Dierum, to the elastic interpretation given in his time to the " days " in the first chapter of Genesis. " It is not probable that God, in inspiring Moses to write a history of the Creation, which was to be believed by ordinary people, would have made him use language the true meaning of which it was hard to discover, and still harder to believe." Three centuries have passed since these wise words were penned, and the reproof which they convey is as much needed now as then.

In near connection with the question of man's origin is that of his antiquity. The existence of his remains, rare as they are everywhere, in deposits older than the Pleistocene or Quaternary Epoch is not proven. This applies to the remarkable fragments found by Dr. Dubois in Java, the character of which, in the judgment of several palæontologists, indicates the nearest approach between man and ape hitherto discovered. But the evidence of the physical relation of these two being conclusive, the exact place of man in the earth's time-record is rendered of subordinate importance.

The theologians have come to their last ditch in contesting that the mental differences between man and the lower animals are fundamental, being differences of kind, and therefore that no gradual process from the mental faculties of the one to those of the other has taken place. This struggle against the application of the theory of Evolution to man's intellectual and spiritual nature will be long and stubborn. It is a matter of life and death to the theologian to show that he has in revelation, and in the world-wide belief of mankind in spiritual existences without, and in a spirit or soul within, evidence of the supernatural. The evolutionist has no such corresponding deep concern. When the argument against him is adduced from the Bible, he can only challenge the ground on which that book is cited as divine authority, or as an authority at all. Granting, for the sake of argument, that a revelation has been made, the writings purporting to contain it must comply with the twofold condition attaching to it, namely, that it makes known matters which the human mind could not, unaided, have found out; and that it embodies those matters in language as to the meaning of which there can be no doubt whatever. If there be any sacred books which comply with these conditions, they have yet to be discovered.

When the argument against the evolutionist is drawn from human testimony, he does not dispute the existence of the belief in a soul and in all the accompanying apparatus of the supernatural; but he calls in the anthropologist to explain how these arose in the barbaric mind.

Meanwhile, let us summarize the evidence which points to the psychical unity between man and the lower life-forms. As stated on p. 187, Mr. Herbert Spencer traces the gradual evolution of consciousness from " the blurred, indeterminate feeling which responds to a single nerve pulsation or shock." There is no trace of a nervous system in the simplest organisms, but this counts for little, because there are also no traces of a mouth, or a stomach, or limbs. In these seemingly structureless creatures every part does everything. The amœba eats and drinks, digests and excretes, manifests " irritability," that is, responds to the various stimuli of its surroundings, and multiplies, without possessing special organs for these various functions. Division of labour arises at a slightly higher stage, when rudimentary organs appear; the development of function and organ going on simultaneously.

Speaking broadly, the functions of living things are threefold: they feed; they reproduce; they respond to their " environment," and it is this last-named function—communication with surroundings

—which is the special work of the nervous system. It was an old Greek maxim that "a man may once say a thing as he would have said it: he cannot say it twice." This is the warrant for transferring a few sentences on the origin of the nerves from my Story of Creation. They are but a meagre abstract of Mr. Spencer's long, but luminous exposition of the subject.

"As every part of an organism is made up of cells, and as the functions govern the form of the cells, the origin of nerves must be due to a modification in cell shape and arrangement, whereby certain tracts or fibres of communication between the body and its surroundings are established.

"But what excited that modification? The all-surrounding medium, without which no life had been, which determined its limits, and *touches* it at every point with its throbs and vibrations. In the beginnings of a primitive layer or skin manifested by creatures a stage above the lowest, unlikenesses would arise, and certain parts, by reason of their finer structure, would be the more readily stimulated by, and the more quickly responsive to, the ceaseless action of the surroundings, the result being that an extra sensitiveness along the lines of least resistance would be set up in those more delicate parts. These, developing, like all things else, by use, would become more and more the selected paths of the impulses, leading, as the molecular waves thrilled them, to structural changes or modification into nerve-cells, and nerve-fibres, of increasing complexity as we ascend the scale of life. The entire nervous system, with its connections; the brain and all the subtle mechanism with which it controls the body; the organs of the senses alike begin as sacs formed by infoldings of the primitive outer skin."

Biologists are agreed that a certain stage in the organization of the nervous system—the germs of which, we saw, are visible in the quivering of an amœba, and probably in plants as well as animals —must be reached before consciousness is manifest. Obscurity still hangs round the stage at which mere irritability passes into sensibility, but so long as the continuity of development is clear, the gradations are of lesser importance. And, for the present purpose, there is no need to descend far in the life-scale; if the psychical connection between man and the mammals immediately beneath him is proven, the connection of the mammals with the lowest invertebrate may be assumed as also established. Speaking only of vertebrates, the brain being, whether in fish or man, the organ of mental phenomena, how far does its structure support or destroy the theory of mental continuity? In Man's Place in Nature, and its invaluable supplement, the second part of the monograph on Hume, this subject is expounded by Huxley with his usual clearness. In the older book he traces the gradual modification of brain in the series of backboned animals. He points out that the brain of a fish is very small compared with the spinal cord into which it is continued, that in reptiles the mass of brain, relatively to the spinal cord, is larger, and still larger in birds, until among the lowest mammals, as the opossums and kangaroos, the brain is so increased in proportion as to be extremely different from that of fish, bird, or reptile. Between these marsupials and the highest or placental mammals, there occurs " the greatest leap anywhere made by Nature in her brain work." Then follows this important statement in favour of continuity.

" As if to demonstrate, by a striking example, the impossibility of erecting any cerebral barrier between man and the apes, Nature has provided us, in the latter animals, with an almost complete series of gradations from brains little higher than that of a Rodent to brains little lower than that of Man." After giving technical descriptions in proof of this, and laying special stress on the presence of the structure known as the " hippocampus minor " in the brain of man as well as of the ape—in the denial of which Owen cut such a sorry figure, Huxley adds:

" So far as cerebral structure goes, therefore, it is clear that Man differs less from the Chimpanzee or the Orang than these do even from the Monkeys, and that the difference between the brains of the Chimpanzee and of Man is almost insignificant when compared with that between the Chimpanzee brain and that of a Lemur. . . . Thus, whatever system of organs be studied, the comparison of their modifica-

tions in the ape series leads to one and the same
result,—that the structural differences which separate
Man from the Gorilla and the Chimpanzee are not so
great as those which separate the Gorilla from the
lower apes. But in enunciating this important truth
I must guard myself against a form of misunderstanding which is very prevalent . . . that the structural differences between man and even the highest
apes are small and insignificant. Let me then distinctly assert, on the contrary, that they are great
and significant; that every bone of a Gorilla bears
marks by which it might be distinguished from the
corresponding bone of a Man; and that, in the present creation, at any rate, no intermediate link bridges
over the gap between *Homo* and *Troglodytes.* It
would be no less wrong than absurd to deny the existence of this chasm; but it is at least equally wrong
and absurd to exaggerate its magnitude, and, resting on the admitted fact of its existence, to refuse to
inquire whether it is wide or narrow. Remember, if
you will, that there is no existing link between Man
and the Gorilla, but do not forget that there is a no
less sharp line of demarcation, a no less complete
absence of any traditional form, between the Gorilla
and the Orang, or the Orang and the Gibbon."

The brains of man and ape being fundamentally
the same in structure, it follows that the functions
which they perform are fundamentally the same.
The large array of facts mustered by a series of
careful observers prove how futile is the argument

which, in his pride of birth, man advances against
psychical continuity. Vain is the search after
boundary lines between reflex action and instinct,
and between instinct and reason. Barriers there are
between man and brute, for articulate speech and
the consequent power to transmit experiences has
set up these, and they remain impassable. " The
potentialities of language, as the vocal symbol of
thought, lay in the faculty of modulating and articu-
lating the voice. The potentialities of writing, as
the visual symbol of thought, lay in the hand that
could draw, and in the mimetic tendency which
we know was gratified by drawing as far back as
the days of Quaternary man " (Huxley's Essays on
Controverted Questions, p. 47). But these specially
human characteristics are no sufficing warrant for
denying that the sensations, emotions, thoughts, and
volitions of man vary in kind from those of the
lower creation. " The essential resemblances in all
points of structure and function, so far as they can
be studied, between the nervous system of man and
that of the dog, leave no reasonable doubt that the
processes which go on in the one are just like those
which take place in the other. In the dog, there can
be no doubt that the nervous matter which lies
between the retina and the muscles undergoes a
series of changes, precisely analogous to those which,
in the man, give rise to sensation, a train of thought,
and volition." This passage occurs in Huxley's
Reply to Mr. Darwin's Critics, which appeared in

the Contemporary Review, 1871, and it may be supplemented by a quotation from the chapter on The Mental Phenomena of Animals in his Hume. " It seems hard to assign any good reason for denying to the higher animals any mental state or process in which the employment of the vocal or visual symbols of which language is composed is not involved; and comparative psychology confirms the position in relation to the rest of the animal world assigned to man by comparative anatomy. As comparative anatomy is easily able to show that, physically, man is but the last term of a long series of forms, which lead, by slow gradations, from the highest mammal to the almost formless speck of living protoplasm, which lies on the shadowy boundary between animal and vegetable life; so, comparative psychology, though but a young science, and far short of her elder sister's growth, points to the same conclusion."

Within recent years the psychologists are doing remarkable work in attacking the problem of the mechanics of mental operations, and already in Europe and America some thirty laboratories have been started for experimental work. The subject is somewhat abstruse for detailed reference here, and it must suffice to say that the psychologist, beginning with observations upon himself, measuring, for example, " the degree of sensibility of his own eye to luminous irritations, or of his own skin to pricking, passes on to like inquiry into the numerical relations between the energy of the stimuli of light, sound, and so forth, and the energy of the sensations which they arouse in the nerve-channels." An excellent summary, with references to the newest authorities on the subject, is given by Prince Kropotkin in the Nineteenth Century of August, 1896.

All this, to the superficial onlooker, seems rank materialism. But we cannot think without a brain any more than we can see without eyes, and any inquiry into the operation of the organ of thought must run on the same lines as inquiry into the operations of any other organ of the body. And the inquiry leaves us at the point whence we began in so far as any light is thrown on the connection between the molecular vibrations in nerve-tissue and the mental processes of which they are the indispensable accompaniment. Changes take place in some of the thousands of millions of brain-cells in every thought that we think, and in every emotion that we feel, but the nexus remains an impenetrable mystery. Nevertheless, if we may not say that the brain secretes thought as we say that the liver secretes bile, we may also not say that the mind is detachable from the nervous system, and that it is an entity independent of it. Were it this, not only would it stand outside the ordinary conditions of development, but it would also maintain the equilibrium which a dose of narcotics or of alcohol, or which starvation and gorging alike rapidly upset.

In his posthumous essay On the Immortality of

the Soul, Hume says: "Matter and spirit are at bottom equally unknown, and we cannot determine what qualities inhere in the one or in the other." That is the conclusion to which the wisest come. And in the ultimate correlation of the physical and psychical lies the hope of arrival at that terminus of unity which was the dream of the ancient Greeks, and to which all inquiry makes approach. How, in these matters, philosophy is at one, is again seen in Huxley's admission that " in respect of the great problems of philosophy, the post-Darwinian generation is, in one sense, exactly where the præ-Darwinian generations were. They remain insoluble. But the present generation has the advantage of being better provided with the means of freeing itself from the tyranny of certain sham solutions."

Science explains, and, in explaining, dissipates the pseudo-mysteries by which man, in his myth-making stage, when conception of the order of the universe was yet unborn, accounted for everything. But she may borrow the Apostle's words, " Behold! I show you a mystery," and give to them a profounder meaning as she confesses that the origin and ultimate destiny of matter and motion; the causes which determine the behaviour of atoms, whether they are arranged in the lovely and varying forms which mark their crystals, or whether they are quivering with the life which is common to the amœba and the man; the conversion of the inorganic into the organic by the green plant, and the relation between nerve-changes and consciousness; are all impenetrable mysteries.

In his speech on the commemoration of the jubilee of his Professorship in the University of Glasgow last year, Lord Kelvin said, " I know no more of electric and magnetic force, or of the relation between ether, electricity, and ponderable matter, or of chemical affinity than I knew and tried to teach my students of natural philosophy fifty years ago in my first session as professor."

This recognition of limitations will content those who seek not " after a sign." For others, that search will continue to have encouragement not only from the theologian, but from the pseudo-scientific who have travelled some distance with the Pioneers of Evolution, but who refuse to follow them further. In each of these there is present the " theological bias " whose varied forms are skilfully analyzed by Mr. Spencer in his chapter under that heading in the Study of Sociology. This explains the attitude of various groups which are severally represented by Mr. St. George Mivart, and the late Dr. W. B. Carpenter; by Professor Sir Geo. G. Stokes, and Mr. Alfred Russel Wallace. The first-named is a Roman Catholic; the second was a Unitarian; the third is an orthodox Churchman, and the fourth, as already seen, is a Spiritualist. In his Genesis of Species, Mr. Mivart contends that " man's body was evolved from pre-existing material (symbolised by the term ' dust of the earth '), and was therefore only derivatively

16

created, i. e., by the operation of secondary laws,"
but that " his soul, on the other hand, was created in
quite a different way . . . by the direct action of
the Almighty (symbolised by the term breathing),"
p. 325. In his Mental Physiology, Dr. Carpenter
postulates an Ego or Will which presides over, without sharing in, the causally determined action of the
other mental functions and their correlated bodily
processes; "an entity which does not depend for its
existence on any play of physical or vital forces, but
which makes these forces subservient to its deter-
minations" (p. 27). Professor Mivart actually cites
St. Augustine and Cardinal Newman as authorities
in support of his theory of the special creation of the
soul. He might with equal effect subpœna Dr.
Joseph Parker or General Booth as authorities. Dr.
Carpenter argued as became a good Unitarian. In
his Gifford Lectures on Natural Theology, Professor
Stokes asserts, drawing "on sources of information
which lie beyond man's natural powers," in other
words, appealing to the Bible, that God made man
immortal and upright, and endowed him with freedom of the will. As, without the exercise of this,
man would have been as a mere automaton, he was
exposed to the temptation of the devil, and fell.
Thereby he became " subject to death like the lower
animals," and by the " natural effect of heredity,"
transmitted the taint of sin to his offspring. The
eternal life thus forfeited was restored by the volun-
tary sacrifice of Christ, but can be secured only to

those who have faith in him. This doctrine, which is no novel one, is known as " conditional immortality." Professor Stokes attaches " no value to the belief in a future life by metaphysical arguments founded on the supposed nature of the soul itself," and he admits that the purely psychic theory which would discard the body altogether in regard to the process of thought is beset by very great difficulties. So he once more has recourse to " sources of information which lie beyond man's natural powers." Following up certain distinctions between " soul " and " spirit " drawn by the Apostle Paul in his tripartite division of man, Professor Stokes, somewhat in keeping with Dr. Carpenter, assumes an " Ego, which, on the one hand, is not to be identified with thought, which may exist while thought is in abeyance, and which may, with the future body of which the Christian religion speaks, be the medium of continuity of thought. . . . What the nature of this body might be we do not know; but we are pretty distinctly informed that it would be something very different from that of our present body, very different in its properties and functions, and yet no less our own than our present body." " Words, words, words," as Hamlet says.

Reference has been made in some fulness to Mr. Wallace's limitations of the theory of natural selection in the case of man's mental faculties. We must now pursue this somewhat in detail, reminding the reader of Mr. Wallace's admission that, " provision-

ally, the laws of variation and natural selection . . .
may have brought about, first, that perfection of
bodily structure in which man is so far above all
other animals, and, in co-ordination with it, the
larger and more developed brain by means of which
he has been able to subject the whole animal and
vegetable kingdoms to his service." But, although
Mr. Wallace rejects the theory of man's special creation as "being entirely unsupported by facts, as
well as in the highest degree improbable," he contends that it does not necessarily follow that "his
mental nature, even though developed *pari passu*
with his physical structure, has been developed by
the same agencies." Then, by the introduction of a
physical analogy which is no analogy at all, he suggests that the agent by which man was upraised
into a kingdom apart bears like relation to natural
selection as the glacial epoch bears to the ordinary
agents of denudation and other changes in producing
new effects which, though continuous with preceding
effects, were not due to the same causes.

Applying this "argument" (drawn from natural
causes), as Mr. Wallace names it, "to the case of
man's intellectual and moral nature," he contends
that such special faculties as the mathematical,
musical, and artistic (is this faculty to be denied the
nest-decorating bower bird?), and the high moral
qualities which have given the martyr his constancy,
the patriot his devotion, and the philanthropist his
unselfishness, are due to a " spiritual essence or na-

ture, superadded to the animal nature of man." We are not told at what stage in man's development this was inserted; whether, once and for all, in " primitive " man, with potentiality of transmission through Palæolithic folk to all succeeding generations; or whether there is special infusion of a " spiritual essence " into every human being at birth.

Any perplexity that might arise at the line thus taken by Mr. Wallace vanishes before the fact, already enlarged upon, that the author of the Malay Archipelago and Island Life has written a book on Miracles and Modern Spiritualism in defence of both. The explanation lies in that duality of mind which, in one compartment, ranks Mr. Wallace foremost among naturalists, and, in the other compartment, places him among the most credulous of Spiritualists.

Despite this, Mr. Wallace has claims to a respectful hearing and to serious reply. Fortunately, he would appear to furnish the refutation to his own argument in the following paragraph from his delightful Contributions to the Theory of Natural Selection:

" From the time when the social and sympathetic feelings came into operation and the intellectual and moral faculties became fairly developed, man would cease to be influenced by natural selection in his physical form and structure. As an animal he would remain almost stationary, the changes in the surrounding universe ceasing to produce in him that powerful modifying effect which they exercise on

other parts of the organic world. But, from the
moment that the form of his body became stationary,
his mind would become subject to those very influences from which his body had escaped; every slight
variation in his mental and moral nature which
should enable him better to guard against adverse
circumstances and combine for mutual comfort and
protection would be preserved and accumulated; the
better and higher specimens of our race would therefore increase and spread, the lower and more brutal
would give way and successively die out, and that
rapid advancement of mental organisation would
occur which has raised the very lowest races of man
so far above the brutes (although differing so little
from some of them in physical structure), and, in con-
junction with scarcely perceptible modifications of
form, has developed the wonderful intellect of the
European races" (pp. 316, 317, Second Edition,
1871).

This argument has suggestive illustration in the
fifth chapter of the Origin of Species. Mr. Darwin
there refers to a remark to the following effect made
by Mr. Waterhouse: " *A part developed in any species
in an extraordinary degree or manner in comparison
with the same part in allied species tends to be highly
variable.*" This applies only where there is unusual
development. " Thus, the wing of a bat is a most
abnormal structure in the class of mammals; but
the rule would not apply here, because the whole
group of bats possesses wings; it would apply only

if some one species had wings developed in a remarkable manner in comparison with the other species of the same genius." And when this exceptional development of any part or organ occurs, we may conclude that the modification has arisen since the period when the several species branched off from the common progenitor of the genus; and this period will seldom be very remote, as species rarely endure for more than one geological period.

How completely this applies to man, the latest product of organic evolution. The brain is that part or organ in him which has been developed " in an extraordinary degree, in comparison with the same part " in other Primates, and which has become *highly variable.* Whatever may have been the favouring causes which secured his immediate progenitors such modification of brain as advanced him in intelligence over " allied species," the fact abides that in this lies the explanation of their after-history; the arrest of the one, the unlimited progress of the other. Increasing intelligence at work through vast periods of time originated and developed those social conditions which alone made possible that progress which, in its most advanced degree, but a small proportion of the race has reached. For in this question of mental differences the contrast is not between man and ape, but between man savage and civilized; between the incapacity of the one to count beyond his fingers, and the capacity of the other to calculate an eclipse of the sun or a transit of Venus.

It would therefore seem that Mr. Wallace should introduce his " spiritual essence, or nature," in the intermediate, and not in the initial stage.

As answer to Mr. Wallace's argument that in their large and well-developed brains, savages " possess an organ quite disproportioned to their requirements," Huxley cites Wallace's own remarks in his paper on Instinct in Man and Animals as to the considerable demands made by the needs of the lower races on their observing faculties which call into play no mean exercise of brain function.

" Add to this," Huxley says, " the knowledge which a savage is obliged to gain of the properties of plants, of the characters and habits of animals, and of the minute indications by which their course is discoverable; consider that even an Australian can make excellent baskets and nets, and neatly fitted and beautifully balanced spears; that he learns to use these so as to be able to transfix a quartern loaf at sixty yards; and that very often, as in the case of the American Indians, the language of a savage exhibits complexities which a well-trained European finds it difficult to master; consider that every time a savage tracks his game, he employs a minuteness of observation, and an accuracy of inductive and deductive reasoning which, applied to other matters, would assure some reputation, and I think one need ask no further why he possesses such a fair supply of brains.". . . But Mr. Wallace's objection " applies quite as strongly to the lower animals.

Surely a wolf must have too much brain, or else how is it that a dog, with only the same quantity and form of brain, is able to develop such singular intelligence? The wolf stands to the dog in the same relation as the savage to the man; and therefore, if Mr. Wallace's doctrine holds good, a higher power must have superintended the breeding up of wolves from some inferior stock, in order to prepare them to become dogs" (Critiques and Addresses, p. 293).

After all is said, perhaps the effective refutation of the belief in a spiritual entity superadded in man is found in the explanation of the origin of that belief which anthropology supplies.

The theory of the origin and growth of the belief in souls and spiritual beings generally, and in a future life, which has been put into coherent form by Spencer and Tylor, is based upon an enormous mass of evidence gathered by travellers among existing barbaric peoples; evidence agreeing in character with that which results from investigations into beliefs of past races in varying stages of culture. Only brief reference to it here is necessary, but the merest outline suffices to show from what obvious phenomena the conception of a soul was derived, a conception of which all subsequent forms are but elaborated copies. As in other matters, crude analogies have guided the barbaric mind in its ideas about spirits and their behaviour. A man falls asleep and dreams certain things; on waking, he believes that these things actually happened; and he therefore concludes that the dead who came to him or to whom he went in his dreams, are alive; that the friend or foe whom he knows to be far away, but with whom he feasted or fought in dreamland, came to him. He sees another man fall into a swoon or trance that may lay him seemingly lifeless for hours or even days; he himself may be attacked by deranging fevers and see visions stranger than those which a healthy person sees; shadows of himself and of objects, both living and not living, follow or precede him and lengthen or shorten in the withdrawing or advancing light; the still water throws back images of himself; the hillsides resound with mocking echoes of his words and of sounds around him; and it is these and allied phenomena which have given rise to the notion of " another self," to use Mr. Spencer's convenient term, or of a number of selves that are sometimes outside the man and sometimes inside him, as to which the barbaric mind is never sure. Outside him, however, when the man is sleeping, so that he must not be awakened, lest this " other self " be hindered from returning; or when he is sick, or in the toils of the medicine-man, who may hold the " other self " in his power, as in the curious soul-trap of the Polynesians—a series of cocoa-nut rings —in which the sorcerer makes believe to catch and detain the soul of an offender or sick person. When Dr. Catat and his companions, MM. Maistre and Foucart were exploring the " Bara " country on the west coast of Madagascar the people suddenly became hostile. On the previous day the travellers, not without difficulty, had photographed the royal family, and now found themselves accused of taking the souls of the natives with the object of selling them when they returned to France. Denial was of no avail; following the custom of the Malagasays, they were compelled to catch the souls, which were then put into a casket, and ordered by Dr. Catat to return to their respective owners (Times, 24th March, 1891).

Although the difference presented by such phenomena and by death is that it is abiding, while they are temporary, to the barbaric mind the difference is in degree, and not in kind. True, the "other self" has left the body, and will never return to it; but it exists, for it appears in dreams and hallucinations, and therefore is believed to revisit its ancient haunts, as well as to tarry often near the exposed or buried body. The nebulous theories which identified the soul with breath, and shadow, and reflection, slowly condensed into theories of semi-substantiality still charged with ethereal conceptions, resulting in the curious amalgam which, in the minds of cultivated persons, whenever they strive to envisage the idea, represents the disembodied soul.

Therefore, in vain may we seek for points of difference in our comparison of primitive ideas of the origin and nature of the soul with the later ideas. The copious literature to which these have given

birth is represented in the bibliography appended to
Mr. Alger's work on Theories of a Future Life, by
4977 books, exclusive of many published since his
list was compiled. Save in refinement of detail such
as a higher culture secures, what is there to choose
between the four souls of the Hidatsa Indians, the
two souls of the Gold Coast natives, and the tripartite
division of man by Rabbis, Platonists, and Paulinists,
which are but the savage other-self " writ large "?
Their common source is in man's general animistic
interpretation of Nature, which is a *vera causa,* super-
seding the need for the assumptions of which Mr.
Wallace's is a type. As an excellent illustration of
what is meant by animism, we may cite what Mr.
Everard im Thurn has to say about the Indians of
Guiana, who are, presumably, a good many steps
removed from so-called " primitive " man.   " The
Indian does not see any sharp line of distinction
such as we see between man and other animals, between one kind of animal and another, or between
animals—man included—and inanimate objects. On
the contrary, to the Indian all objects, animate and
inanimate, seem exactly of the same nature, except
that they differ in the accident of bodily form. Every
object in the whole world is a being, consisting of
a body and spirit, and differs from every other object in no respect except that of bodily form, and in
the greater or lesser degree of brute power and brute
cunning consequent on the difference of bodily form
and bodily habits. Our next step, therefore, is to

note that animals, other than men, and even inanimate objects, have spirits which differ not at all in
kind from those of men."

The importance of the evidence gathered by anthropology in support of man's inclusion in the general theory of evolution is ever becoming more manifest. For it has brought witness to continuity in organic development at the point where a break has
been assumed, and driven home the fact that if
Evolution operates anywhere, it operates everywhere.
And operates, too, in such a way that every part co-
operates in the discharge of a universal process.
Hence it meets the divisions which mark opposition
to it by the transcendent power of unity.

Until the past half-century, man excepted himself, save in crude and superficial fashion, from that
investigation which, for long periods, he has made
into the earth beneath him and the heavens above
him. This tardy inquiry into the history of his own
kind, and its place in the order and succession of life,
as well as its relation to the lower animals, between
whom and itself, as has been shown, the barbaric
mind sees much in common, is due, so far as Christendom is concerned (and the like cause applies,
mutatis mutandis, in non-Christian civilized communities), to the subjection of the intellect to pre-con-
ceived theories based on the authority accorded to
ancient legends about man. These legends, invested
with the sanctity with which time endows the past,
finally became integral parts of sacred literatures, to

question which was as superfluous as it was impious. Thus it has come to pass that the only being competent to inquire into his own antecedents has looked at his history through the distorting prism of a mythopœic past!

Perhaps, in the long run, the gain has exceeded the loss. For, in the precedence of study of other sciences more remote from man's "business and bosom," there has been rendered possible a more dispassionate treatment of matters charged with profounder issues. Since the Church, however she may conveniently ignore the fact as concession after concession is wrung from her, has never slackened in jealousy of the advance of secular knowledge, it was well for human progress that those subjects of inquiry which affected orthodox views only indirectly were first prosecuted. The brilliant discoveries in astronomy, to which the Copernican theory gave impetus, although they displaced the earth from its assumed supremacy among the bodies in space, did not apparently affect the doctrine of the supremacy of man as the centre of Divine intervention, as the creature for whom the great scheme of redemption had been formulated " in the counsels of the Trinity," and the tragedy of the self-sacrifice of God the Son enacted on earth. The surrender or negacion of any fundamental dogma of Christian theology was not involved in the abandonment of the statement in the Bible as to the dominant position of the earth in relation to the sun and other self-luminous stars.

To our own time the increase of knowledge concerning the myriads of sidereal systems which revolve through space is not held to be destructive of those dogmas, but held, rather, to supply material for speculation as to the probable extension of Divine paternal government throughout the universe. And, although, as coming nearer home, with consequent greater chance of intrusion of elements of friction, the like applies to the discoveries of geology. Apart from intellectual apathy, which explains much, the impact of these discoveries on traditional beliefs was softened by the buffers which a moderating spirit of criticism interposed in the shape of superficial " reconciliations " emptying the old cosmogony of all its poetry, and therefore of its value as a key to primitive ideas, and converting it into bastard science. Thus a temporary, because artificial, unity, was set up. But with the evidence supplied by study of the ancient life whose remains are imbedded in the fossil-yielding strata, that unity is shivered. In a Scripture that " cannot be broken " there was read the story of conflict and death æons before man appeared. Between this record, and that which spoke of pain and death as the consequences of man's disobedience to the frivolous prohibition of an anthropomorphic God, there is no possible reconciliation.

To the evidence from fossiliferous beds was added evidence from old river-gravels and limestone caverns. The relics extracted from the stalagmitic

deposits in Kent's Hole, near Torquay, had lain unheeded for some years save as " curios," when M.
Boucher des Perthes saw in the worked flints of a
somewhat rougher type which he found mingled with
the bones of rhinoceroses, cave-bears, mammoths, or
woolly-haired elephants, and other mammals in the
" drift" or gravel-pits of Abbeville, in Picardy, the
proofs of man's primitive savagery, so far as Western
Europe was concerned.   The presence of these
rudely-chipped flints had been noticed by M. de
Perthes in 1839, but he could not persuade savants
to admit that human hands had shaped them, until
these doubting Thomases saw for themselves like
implements *in situ* at a depth of seventeen feet from
the original surface of the ground.   That was in
1858: a year before the publication of the Origin of
Species.   Similar materials have been unearthed
from every part of the globe habitable once or in-
habited now.   They confirm the speculations of Lucretius as to a universal makeshift with stone, bone,
horn, and such-like accessible or pliable substances
during the ages that preceded the discovery of
metals.   Therefore, the existence of a Stone Age at
one period or another where now an Age of Iron
(following an Age of Bronze) prevails, is an established canon of archæological science.   From this
follows the inference that man's primitive condition
was that which corresponds to the lowest type ex-
tant, the Australian and Papuan; that the further
back inquiry is pushed such culture as exists is found

to have been preceded by barbarism; and that the savage races of to-day represent not a degradation to which man, as the result of a fall from primeval purity and Eden-like ease, has sunk, but a condition out of which all races above the savage have emerged.

While Prehistoric Archæology, with its enormous mass of *material* remains gathered from " dens and caves of the earth," from primitive work-shops, from rude tombs and temples, thus adds its testimony to the " great cloud of witnesses "; *immaterial* remains, potent as embodying the thought of man, are brought by the twin sciences of Comparative Mythology and Folklore, and Comparative Theology—remains of paramount value, because existing to this day in hitherto unsuspected form, as survivals in beliefs and rites and customs. Readers of Tylor's Primitive Culture, with its wealth of facts and their significance; and of Lyall's Asiatic Studies, wherein is described the making of myths to this day in the heart of India; need not be told how the slow zigzag advance of man in material things has its parallel in the stages of his intellectual and spiritual advance all the world over; from the lower animism to the higher conception of deity; from bewildering guesses to assuring certainties. To this mode of progress no civilized people has been the exception, as notably in the case of the Hebrews, was once thought—" the correspondence between the old Israelitic and other archaic forms of theology extending to details."

While, therefore, the discoveries of astronomers

17

and geologists have been disintegrating agencies
upon old beliefs, the discoveries classed under the
general term Anthropological are acting as more
powerful solvents on every opinion of the past.
Showing on what mythical foundation the story of
the fall of man rests, Anthropology has utterly de-
molished the *raison d'être* of the doctrine of his redemption—the keystone of the fabric. It has penetrated the mists of antiquity, and traced the myth of
a forfeited Paradise, of the Creation, the Deluge, and
other legends, to their birthplaces in the valley of
the Euphrates or the uplands of Persia; legends
whose earliest inscribed records are on Accadian
tablets, or in the scriptures of Zarathustra. It has
in the spirit of the commended Bereans, " searched "
those and other scriptures, finding therein legends
of founders of ancient faiths cognate to those which
in the course of the centuries gathered round Jesus
of Nazareth; it has collated the rites and ceremonies
of many a barbaric theology with those of old-world
religions—Brahmanic, Buddhistic, Christian—and
found only such differences between them as are
referable to the higher or the lower culture. For
the history of superstitions is included in the history
of beliefs; the superstitions being the germ-plasm of
which all beliefs above the lowest are the modified
products. Belief incarnates itself in word or act. In
the one we have the charm, the invocation, and the
dogma; in the other the ritual and ceremony. " A
ritual system," Professor Robertson Smith remarks,

" must always remain materialistic, even if its materialism is disguised under the cloak of mysticism." And it is with the incarnated ideas, uninfluenced by the particular creed in connection with which it finds them, that anthropology deals. Its method is that of biology. Without bias, without assumptions of relative truth or falsity, the anthropologist searches into origins, traces variations, compares and classifies, and relates the several families to one ordinal group. He must be what was said of Dante, " a theologian to whom no dogma is foreign." Unfortunately, this method, whose application to the physical sciences is unchallenged, is, when applied to beliefs, regarded as one of attack, instead of being one of explanation. But this should not deter; and if in analyzing a belief we kill a superstition, this does but show what mortality lay at its core. For error cannot survive dissection. Moreover, as John Morley puts it, " to tamper with veracity is to tamper with the vital force of human progress." Therefore, delivering impartial judgment, the verdict of anthropology upon the whole matter is that the claims of Christian theologians to a special and divine origin of their religion are refuted by the accordant evidence of the latest utterances of a science whose main concern is with the origin, nature, and destiny of man.

The extension of the comparative method to the various products of man's intellectual and spiritual nature is the logical sequence to the adoption of that method throughout every department of the universe. Of course it starts with the assumption of differences in things, else it would be superfluous. But it equally starts with the assumption of resemblances, and in every case it has brought out the fact that the differences are superficial, and that the resemblances are fundamental.

All this bears closely on Huxley's work. The impulse thereto has come largely from the evidence focussed in Man's Place in Nature, evidence of which the material of the writings of his later years is the expansion. The cultivation of intellect and character had always been a favourite theme with him, and the interest was widened when the passing of Mr. Forster's Elementary Education Act in 1870 brought the problem of popular culture to the front. The wave of enthusiasm carried a group of distinguished liberal candidates to the polls, and Huxley was elected a member of the School Board for London. Then, although in not so acute a form as now, the religious difficulty was the sole cause of any serious division, and Huxley's attitude therein puzzled a good many people because he advocated the retention of the Bible in the schools. Those who should have known him better thought that he was (to quote from one of his letters to the writer) " a hypocrite, or simply a fool." " But," he adds, " my meaning was that the mass of the people should not be deprived of the one great literature which is open to them, nor shut out from the perception of its place in the whole past history of civilised mankind."

He lamented, as every thoughtful person must lament, the decay of Bible reading in this generation, while, at the same time, he advocated the more strenuously its detachment from the glosses and theological inferences which do irreparable injury to a literature whose value cannot be overrated.

For Huxley was well read in history, and therefore he would not trust the clergy as interpreters of the Bible. After repeating in the Prologue to his Essays on Controverted Questions what he had said about the book in his article on the School Boards in Critiques and Addresses, he adds, " I laid stress on the necessity of placing such instruction in lay hands; in the hope and belief that it would thus gradually accommodate itself to the coming changes of opinion; that the theology and the legend would drop more and more out of sight, while the perennially interesting historical, literary, and ethical contents would come more and more into view."

Subsequent events have justified neither the hope nor the belief. Had Huxley lived to see that all the sectaries, while quarrelling as to the particular dogmas which may be deduced from the Bible, agree in refusing to use it other than as an instrument for the teaching of dogma, he would probably have come to see that the only solution in the interests of the young, is its exclusion from the schools. Never has any collection of writings, whose miscellaneous, unequal, and often disconnected character is obscured by the common title " Bible " which covers them, had such need for deliverance from the so-called "believers" in it. Its value is only to be realized in the degree that theories of its inspiration are abandoned. Then only is it possible to treat it like any other literature of the kind; to discriminate between the coarse and barbaric features which evidence the humanness of its origin, and the loftier features of its later portions which also evidence how it falls into line with other witnesses of man's gradual ethical and spiritual development.

Huxley's breadth of view, his sympathy with every branch of culture, his advocacy of literary in unison with scientific training, fitted him supremely for the work of the School Board, but its demands were too severe on a man never physically strong, and he was forced to resign. However, he was thereby set free for other work, which could be only effectively done by exchanging the arena for the study. The earliest important outcome of that relief was the monograph on Hume, published in 1879, and the latest was the Romanes lecture on Evolution and Ethics, which was delivered in the Sheldonian Theatre at Oxford on the 18th of May, 1893. Between the two lie a valuable series of papers dealing with the Evolution of Theology and cognate subjects. In all these we have the application of the theory of Evolution to the explanation of the origin of beliefs and of the basis of morals. To quote the saying attributed to Liebnitz, both Spencer and Huxley, and all who follow them, care for " science only because it enables them to speak with authority in philosophy and religion." In a letter to the writer, wherein Huxley refers to his retirement from official life, he says:—

I was so ill that I thought with Hamlet, " the rest is silence." But my wiry constitution has unexpectedly weathered the storm, and I have every reason to believe that with renunciation of the devil and all his works (i. e., public speaking, dining, and being dined, etc.) my faculties may be unimpaired for a good spell yet, And whether my lease is long or short, I mean to devote them to the work I began in the paper on the Evolution of Theology.

That essay was first published in two sections in the Nineteenth Century, 1886, and was the sequel to the eighth chapter of his Hume. The Romanes Lecture supplemented the last chapter of that book. All these are accessible enough to render superfluous any abstract of their contents. But the tribute due to David Hume, who may well-nigh claim place among the few but fit company of Pioneers, warrants reference to his anticipation of accepted theories of the origin of belief in spiritual beings in his Natural History of Religion, published in 1757. He says: " There is an universal tendency among mankind to conceive all beings like themselves, and to transfer to every object those qualities with which they are familiarly acquainted, and of which they are intimately conscious. . . . The *unknown causes* which continually employ their thought, appearing always in the same aspect, are all apprehended to be of the same kind or species. Nor is it long before we ascribe to them thought, and reason, and passion, and sometimes even the limbs and figures of men, in order to bring them nearer to a resemblance with ourselves." In his address to the Sorbonne on The Successive Advances of the Human Mind, delivered in 1750, Turgot expresses the same idea, touching, as John Morley says in his essay on that statesman, "the root of most of the wrong thinking that has been as a manacle to science."

The foregoing, and passages of a like order, are made by Huxley the text of his elaborations of the several stages of theological evolution, the one note of all of which is the continuity of belief in supernatural intervention. But more important than the decay of that belief which is the prelude to decay of belief in deity itself as commonly defined, is the resulting transfer of the foundation of morals, in other words, of motives to conduct, from a theological to a social base. Theology is not morality; indeed, it is, too often, immorality. It is concerned with man's relations to the gods in whom he believes; while morals are concerned with man's relations to his fellows. The one looks heavenward, wondering what dues shall be paid the gods to win their smiles or ward off their frowns. In old Rome *sanctitas* or holiness, was, according to Cicero, "the knowledge of the rites which had to be performed." These done, the gods were expected to do their part. So in new Rome, when the Catholic has attended mass, his share in the contract is ended. Worship and sacrifice, as mere acts toward supernatural beings, may be consonant with any number of lapses in conduct. Morality, on the other hand, looks earthward, and is prompted to action solely by what is due from a man to his fellow-men, or from his fellow-men to him. Its foundation therefore is not in supernatural beliefs, but in social instincts. All sin is thus resolved into an anti-social act: a wrong done by man to man.

This is not merely readjustment; it is revolution. For it is the rejection of theology with its appeals to human obligation to deity, and to man's hopes of future reward or fears of future punishment; and it is the acceptance of wholly secular motives as incentives to right action. Those motives, having their foundation in the physical, mental, and moral results of our deeds, rest on a stable basis. No longer interlaced with the unstable theological, they neither abide nor perish with it. And one redeeming feature of our time is that the churches are beginning to see this, and to be effected by it. John Morley caustically remarks that " the efforts of the heterodox have taught them to be better Christians than they were a hundred years ago." Certain extremists excepted, they are keeping dogma in the background, and are laying stress on the socialism which it is contended was at the heart of the teaching of Jesus. Wisely, if not very consistently, they are seeking alliance with the liberal movements whose aim is the " abolition of privilege." The lib-

eral theologians, in the face of the varying ethical
standards which mark the Old Testament and the
New, no longer insist on the absoluteness of moral
codes, and so fall into line with the evolutionist in
his theory of their relativeness. For society in its
advance from lower to higher conceptions of duty,
completely reverses its ethics, looking back with
horror on that which was once permitted and unquestioned.

It is with this checking of " the ape and tiger,"
and this fostering of the " angel " in man, that Huxley dealt in his Romanes Lecture. There was much
unintelligent, and some wilful, misunderstanding of
his argument, else a prominent Catholic biologist
would hardly have welcomed it as a possible prelude
to Huxley's submission to the Church. Yet the
reasoning was clear enough, and in no wise contra-
vened the application of Evolution to morals. Huxley showed that Evolution is both *cosmical* and *ethical.*
Cosmic Evolution has resulted in the universe with
its non-living and living contents, and since, dealing with the conditions which obtain on our planet,
there is not sufficient elbow-room or food for all the
offspring of living things, the result is a furious
struggle in which the strong win and transmit their
advantages to their descendants. Nature is wholly
selfish; the race is to the swift, and the battle to the
strong.

But there are limits set to that struggle by man
in the substitution, also within limits, of social prog-

ress for cosmic progress. In this *Ethical Evolution* selfishness is so far checked as to permit groups of human beings to live together in amity, recognising certain common rights, which restrain the self-regarding impulses. For, in the words of Marcus Aurelius, " that which is not good for the swarm is not good for the bee " (Med., vi, 54). Huxley aptly likens this counter-process to the action of a gardener in dealing with a piece of waste ground. He stamps out the weeds, and plants fragrant flowers and useful fruits. But he must not relax his efforts, otherwise the weeds will return, and the untended plants will be choked and perish. So in conduct. For the common weal, in which the unit shares, thus blending the selfish and the unselfish motives, men check their natural impulses. The emotions and affections which they share with the lower social animals, only in higher degree, are co-operative, and largely help the development of family, tribal, and national life. But once let these we weakened, and society becomes a bear-garden. Force being the dominant factor in life, the struggle for existence revives in all its primitive violence, and atavism asserts its power. Therefore, although he do the best that in him lies, man can only set limits to that struggle, for the ethical process is an integral part of the cosmic powers, " just as the ' governor ' in a steam-engine is part of the mechanism of the engine." As with society, so with its units: there is no truce in the contest. Dr. Plimmer, an eminent bacteriologist, describes to the writer the action of a kind of yeast upon a species of Daphnia, or water-flea. Metschnikoff observed that these yeast-cells, which enter with the animal's food, penetrate the intestines, and get into the tissues. They are there seized upon by the leukocytes, which gather round the invaders in larger fashion, as if seemingly endowed with consciousness, so marvellous is the strategy. If they win, the Daphnia recovers; if they lose, it dies. "In a similar manner in ourselves certain leukocytes (phagocytes) accumulate at any point of invasion, and pick up the living bacteria," and in the success or failure of their attack lies the fate of man. Which things are fact as well as allegory; and time is on the side of the bacteria. For as our life is but a temporary arrest of the universal movement toward dissolution, so naught in our actions can arrest the destiny of our kind. Huxley thus puts it in the concluding sentences of his Preface—written in July, 1894, one year before his death—to the reissue of Evolution and Ethics:

"That man, as a 'political animal,' is susceptible of a vast amount of improvement, by education, by instruction, and by the application of his intelligence to the adaptation of the conditions of life to his higher needs, I entertain not the slightest doubt. But, so long as he remains liable to error, intellectual or moral; so long as he is compelled to be perpetually on guard against the cosmic forces, whose ends are not his ends, without and within himself; so long as he is haunted by inexpugnable memories and hopeless aspirations; so long as the recognition of his intellectual limitations forces him to acknowledge his incapacity to penetrate the mystery of existence; the prospect of attaining untroubled happiness, or of a state which can, even remotely, deserve the title of perfection, appears to me to be as misleading an illusion as ever was dangled before the eyes of poor humanity. And there have been many of them. That which lies before the human race is a constant struggle to maintain and improve, in opposition to the State of Nature, the State of Art of an organised polity; in which, and by which, man may develop a worthy civilisation, capable of maintaining and constantly improving itself, until the evolution of our globe shall have entered so far upon its downward course that the cosmic process resumes its sway; and, once more, the State of Nature prevails over the surface of our planet."

But only those of low ideals would seek in this impermanence of things excuse for inaction; or worse, for self-indulgence. The world will last a very long time yet, and afford scope for battle against the wrongs done by man to man. Even were it and ourselves to perish to-morrow, our duty is clear while the chance of doing it may be ours. Clifford,—dead before his prime, before the rich promise of his genius had its full fruitage,—speaking of the inevitable end of the earth " and all the consciousness of men " reminds us, in his essay on The First and

Last Catastrophe, that we are helped in facing the fact "by the words of Spinoza: 'The free man thinks of nothing so little as of death, and his wisdom is a meditation not of death but of life.'" "Our interest," Clifford adds, "lies with so much of the past as may serve to guide our actions in the present, and to intensify our pious allegiance to the fathers who have gone before us and the brethren who are with us; and our interest lies with so much of the future as we may hope will be appreciably affected by our good actions now. Do I seem to say, 'Let us eat and drink, for to-morrow we die?' Far from it; on the contrary I say, 'Let us take hands and help, for this day we are alive together.'"

Evolution and Ethics was Huxley's last important deliverance, since the completion of his reply to Mr. Balfour's "quaintly entitled" Foundations of Belief was arrested by his death on the 30th of June, 1895.

In looking through the Collected Essays, which represent his non-technical contributions to knowledge, there may be regret that throughout his life circumstances were against his doing any piece of long-sustained work, such as that which, for example, the affluence and patience of Darwin permitted him to do. But until Huxley's later years, and, indeed, through broken health to the end, his work outside official demands had to be done fitfully and piecemeal, or not at all. Notwithstanding this, it has the unity which is inspired by a central idea. The

application of the theory of evolution all round im-
parts a quality of relation to subjects seemingly diverse. And this comes out clearly and strongly in
the more orderly arrangement of the material in the
new issue of Collected Essays.

These show what an omnivorous reader he was;
how well equipped in classics, theology, and general
literature, in addition to subjects distinctly his own.
He sympathized with every branch of culture. As
contrasted with physical science, he said, " Nothing
would grieve me more than to see literary training
other than a very prominent branch of education."
One corner of his library was filled with a strange
company of antiquated books of orthodox type; this
he called " the condemned cell." When looking at
the " strange bedfellows " that slept on the shelves,
the writer asked Huxley what author had most influenced a style whose clearness and vigour, nevertheless, seems unborrowed; and he at once named
the masculine and pelluccid Leviathan of Hobbes. He
had the happy faculty of rapidly assimilating what he
read; of clearly grasping an opponent's standpoint;
and what is a man's salvation nowadays, freedom
from that curse of specialism which kills all sense of
proportion, and reduces its slave to the level of the
machine-hand that spends his life in making the
heads of screws. He believed in " scepticism as the
highest duty, and in blind faith as the one unpardon-
able sin." " And," he adds, " it cannot be otherwise,
for every great advance in natural knowledge has

involved the absolute rejection of authority, the cher-
ishing of the keenest scepticism, the annihilation of
the spirit of blind faith; and the most ardent votary
of science holds his firmest convictions, not because
the men he most venerates holds them; not because
their verity is testified by portents and wonders; but
because his experience teaches him that whenever
he chooses to bring these convictions into contact
with their primary source, Nature—whenever he
thinks fit to test them by appealing to experiment
and to observation—Nature will confirm them. The
man of science has learned to believe in justification,
not by faith, but by verification." Therefore he
nursed no illusions; would not say that he knew
when he did not or could not know, and bidding us
follow the evidence whithersoever it leads us, remains the surest-footed guide of our time. Such
leadership is his, since he has gone on "from strength
to strength." The changes in the attitude of man
toward momentous questions which new evidence
and the *zeit-geist* have effected, have been approaches
to the position taken by Huxley since he first caught
the public ear. His deep religious feeling kept him
in sympathetic touch with his fellows. Ever present
to him was " that consciousness of the limitation of
man, that sense of an open secret which he cannot
penetrate, in which lies the essence of all religion."
In one of his replies to a prominent exponent of
the Comtian philosophy, that " incongruous mixture
of bad science with eviscerated papistry," as he calls

it, Huxley protests against the idea that the teaching of science is wholly negative.

> I venture, he says, to count it an improbable suggestion that any one who has graduated in all the faculties of human relationships; who has taken his share in all the deep joys and deeper anxieties which cling about them, who has felt the burden of young lives entrusted to his care, and has stood alone with his dead before the abyss of the Eternal—has never had a thought beyond negative criticism.

That is the Agnostic position as he defined it; an attitude, not a creed; and if he refused to affirm, he equally refused to deny.

Thus have the Pioneers of Evolution, clear-sighted and sure-footed, led us by ways undreamed-of at the start to a goal undreamed-of by the earliest among them. To have halted on the route when the graver difficulties of the road began would have made the journey futile, and have left their followers in the wilds. Evolution, applied to everything up to man, but stopping at the stage when he appears, would have remained a fascinating study, but would not have become a guiding philosophy of life. It is in the extension of its processes as explanation of all that appertains to mankind that its abiding value consists. That extension was inevitable. The old theologies of civilized races, useful in their day, because answering, however imperfectly, to permanent needs of human nature, no longer suffice. Their dogmas are traced as the lineal descendants of barbaric conceptions; their ritual is becoming an archæ-

18

ological curiosity. They have no answer to the questions propounded by the growing intelligence of our time; neither can they satisfy the emotions which they but feebly discipline. Their place is being slowly, but surely, and more effectively, filled by a theory which, interpreting the "mighty sum of things," substitutes clear conceptions of unbroken order and relation between phenomena, in place of hazy conceptions of intermittent interferences; a theory which gives more than it takes away. For if men are deprived of belief in the pseudo-mysteries coined in a pre-scientific age, their wonder is fed, and their inquiry is stimulated, by the consciousness of the impenetrable mysteries of the Universe.

INDEX.

THE END.